Praise for *Cultivating Competence*

What does it mean to lead right now? To what extent are we paying attention to the learning and formation needed for leadership? Whether you are a leader yourself, or someone who is responsible for forming ministerial leaders, Drummond offers her readers helpful ways to think about how thoughtful and impactful leadership must be cultivated in the twenty-first century. Now more than ever, we need to be intentional about how we form ourselves and the next generation of ministerial leaders.

—David M. Mellott, president and professor of theological formation, Christian Theological Seminary, Indianapolis, and author of *Finding Your Way in Seminary: What to Expect, How to Thrive*

Sarah Drummond's book reminds us of the essentialness of ongoing and balanced clergy leadership development as we lean into the idea that there is a consistent need for preparedness in a world where change is constant. She encourages leaders to live within the awe and wonder of a Risen Savior and the illumination of the Holy Spirit. She highlights the necessity of being humble, open to learning, knowing it is impossible to know everything but when intentional, it is possible to discover more ways to lead, to inspire, to support, to be curious, and to have a healthy and catalytic awareness that nourishes ministry, staff, and mission.

—Gina C. Jacobs-Strain, General Secretary, American Baptist Churches USA

Provocative and perspicuous, one of the leading authorities on leadership in ministry has written an excellent introduction to the trefoil model of leadership. Drawing on a wide range of literature and her own experiences, Drummond invites those in all phases of ministerial formation—including those in ministry—as well as those who train them, to consider how leadership can be cultivated. The book deserves wide readership.

—Gregory E. Sterling, dean, Yale Divinity School

CULTIVATING COMPETENCE

CULTIVATING COMPETENCE

THE MINISTRY OF LEADERSHIP DEVELOPMENT

SARAH B. DRUMMOND

FORTRESS PRESS
Minneapolis

CULTIVATING COMPETENCE
The Ministry of Leadership Development

30 29 28 27 26 25 1 2 3 4 5 6 7 8 9

Library of Congress Control Number: 2024055039 (print)

Cover image: Oil pastel mountain background
Cover design: Hannah Katanic

Print ISBN: 978-1-5064-9625-2
eBook ISBN: 978-1-5064-9626-9

For Janet Hatfield Legro

My first and best ministry teacher

CONTENTS

PREFACE

College writing instructors assume that students must have learned the basics of how to write in high school. A riverboat guide takes for granted that those who signed up for the trip they are leading know how to swim. Similarly, institutional leaders believe that constituents with educations, work experience, and respectable standing in the community have acquired some understanding of leadership.

Ask any college writing instructor or riverboat guide today whether these assumptions of prior knowledge always pan out, and they will likely say that expectations of a common set of understandings about what kind of preparation is necessary for an undertaking vary immensely, person to person, community to community. Ask any institutional leader who seeks to build coalitions and share authority if the people they empower know how to lead, and they are sure to describe a varied mix of individuals—some gifted but untrained, others confident in their abilities yet lacking fundamental skills in bringing a community together.

Instead of bemoaning their students' lack of prior knowledge, educators across fields must take up the task of teaching what, one might argue, should have already been learned. Leadership is no different. Leaders today must add to their already extensive portfolios the responsibility of providing leadership development. Whether their "students" in such endeavors believe they have much to learn or not, gone are the days when leaders could convince themselves that all those whom they seek to empower have adequate prior knowledge to accomplish the work that needs to be done.

To cultivate competence in the leaders with whom power can be shared and a community strengthened might sound like an unambitious goal. When a person describes a technician as "competent," they are not saying that technician is "excellent" or "superior." Terms like *excellent* and *superior* are meaningless, however, in that they refer to the technician's place on a hierarchy: excellent compared to what? Superior to whom? *Competence* suggests someone who can do the job, and that is a lofty aspiration for a leader in today's complicated and quickly changing culture.

A competent leader not only has the capacity to complete work but has the attitude and disposition to do so when times are tough and over the long haul. Beyond the ability to carry out the work assigned, the ideals toward which a leader—and leadership-development teacher—must aspire is a combination of wonder and wherewithal. The leader who finds group dynamics fascinating rather than exhausting will find endless sources of energy in their work. The one who commits to doing what needs to be done, until it is done, will have more success in a day when few leadership challenges offer easy fixes.

The first two chapters of this book lay the groundwork for the argument that old assumptions about how much attention leaders must pay to developing those they are empowering with authority must be set aside. Leadership has become too complicated to allow for institutions to hand it over to those who think they are "finished" with development.

The book then provides a theoretical framework that leaders can use to design a curriculum of sorts for themselves and those under their authority. That framework will make a sustainable practice of leadership development possible for self and stakeholders, so that leaders might add the development of other leaders to their portfolios of responsibilities without adding overwhelmingly to their workloads. The last chapter offers a series of examples for employing the theoretical framework for self, student, and building up teams of leaders.

Institutions demand that leaders attend to a vast array of concerns on a daily basis. In an increasingly diverse, wired, and fast-paced leadership landscape, where problems are deep-seated and complicated, no one can manage leadership alone. Leaders must attend to their own leadership development just to keep their heads above water. They must also delegate their authority and entrust it to those around them. Those entrusted with leadership find their work in an institution or community to be more meaningful and engaging. Sharing leadership from the middle is the ideal. That said, handing over authority to those who lack adequate preparation can cause harm to the community. It can also burn out individuals who could have contributed meaningfully to the community over years or decades. Delegation without preparation represents a failure of a leader to protect a community's assets.

The institutional leader must model that leadership can and must be learned over time, through various disciplines that all start with taking leadership seriously. Then, they must provide opportunities—with however light a touch leads to positive results—for those in their care to grow in leadership. They must assume that even those who walk in the door with knowledge and experience are not "ready" for leadership today, as it is changing rapidly for everyone.

This book provides a resource for those who are coming to understand that high-school-level writing instruction is insufficient for higher learning, basic swimming skills will not suffice when waters are rising, and there is no such thing as a natural-born leader. Operating from the assumption that all have much to learn and that learning is wondrous and fun will—if nothing else—cause leaders to feel less crazy when they find their work to be hard and the challenges of the day to be more than anyone bargained for.

Leaders across fields face intense conflict. One of the most effective buffers against the winds of change is wise and prepared colleagues who share their mission and will not allow it to be toppled. The Christian tradition values strength in numbers among leaders; Jesus called twelve, after all, not one. When the going gets tough, leaders who choose to go it alone are unlikely to hold on to their roles for long. Instead, they must empower, educate, and deploy those who surround them in order not just to stay in leadership but to move the organization, and eventually the culture, in a life-giving direction. This book provides leaders with a resource for cultivating intersecting circles of capable colleagues to further their institutions' work together. Through leadership development, they pool the community's resources and ensure its mission will endure after the leader has moved on.

Part I

Insufficiency

The Myth that Leadership Development Just Happens

CHAPTER ONE

The Old Way Was No Way

MINISTRY IS LEADERSHIP. Ministry includes leadership. Ministry results in leadership.

No matter which statement above happens to be true, the connection between ministry and leadership cannot be dismissed. Ministers bring faith communities together. They interpret the times and offer theological thought leadership. They guide individuals and families in moral reasoning on matters both public and personal. Competent ministers are leaders. In fact, they cannot be deemed competent for ministry if leadership is something they do not do, or do not do well.

Ministerial leadership development cultivates and hones inner charisms and outward practices toward leadership's improvement. Given how unlikely a minister's success would be if the minister were not a good leader, leadership development merits serious reflection. Some might think that the main reason leadership is largely ignored by theological educators is that the theological education system lacks resources and knowledge about how to teach leadership. Because educators do not know what to do, they—as people who are smart for a living—behave as though it need not be done.

When theological educators abdicate responsibility for ensuring students learn to lead, they say, through their actions, that ministerial leadership is best learned on the job. Relatedly, their neglect suggests, "Either you've got it, or you don't." Both assumptions and assertions are partly true. Experience is a great teacher, and gifts for engaging people and reading situations make leadership learning easier. "Easier," however, will not cut it in a time of rapid, confusing changes in the leadership institutions need.

Anxiety reigns across professions regarding leaders' readiness to face seemingly insurmountable challenges. When professionals are anxious, simple and singular solutions appear all the more tantalizing. What leadership development requires, however, is not an easy answer, but an array of interventions that require time, resources, and attention.

The Nature of Ministerial Leadership and Its Cultivation

Many professions call for care for individuals, families, and communities through provision of guidance, meaning-making, and ritual—from mayors, to school principals, to presidents of parent-teacher associations. The term *ministry* refers to a life of service to something beyond human spheres of influence. The minister's leadership follows the guidance of faith in that which is ineffably greater than human beings. Ministers hold themselves accountable to a higher power which they understand to have a will that is only knowable in part in this life.

Christian ministers' core motivation is to seek out and follow the will of a transcendent force or being: God. By this definition, anyone and everyone can be a minister if they choose to frame their lives as falling under the will of this divine other. Ministry is a full-time occupation for some. For others, it takes place separately from their compensated employment. For anyone called to it, ministry is a way of moving through the world—countercultural in a work-for-pay world. Ministry takes many shapes in the lives of those called to it. Not all persons of faith understand themselves to be ministers, but the Protestant Reformation and other movements in Christian history opened possibilities for numerous formulations for ministerial identities.

Consider the Venn diagram in Figure 1.1, which suggests that God is at the center of the Christian's life, and their ministry—the manner in which they join Jesus in making God's vision real—emerges out of God's will. Also emerging from God-at-center are their work for pay and the way they live their lives, such as how they treat people and care for the earth.

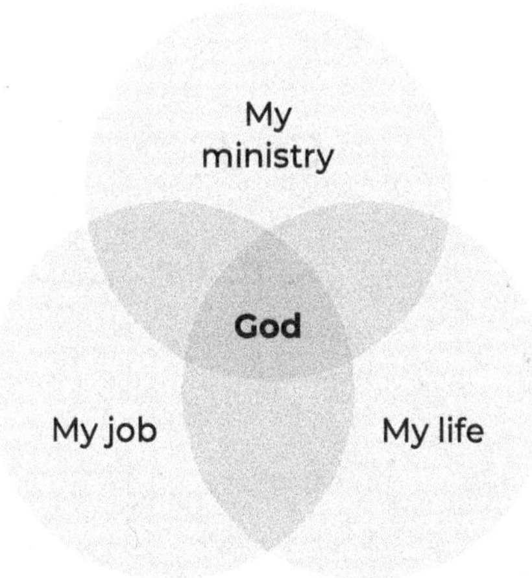

Figure 1.1.

In the lives of some people, the three circles overlap entirely, in ways that are sometimes healthy and sometimes unhealthy. Healthy: a sense that a person's vocation is so fully alive in their work that fulfilling their job's obligations enacts who they are in their most natural state. Unhealthy: when times are tough in a job—as they are bound to be sometimes—a person seeking to carry out their call from God senses that their whole life, and their relationship with the divine, is falling apart. With God at the center, however, proportions of overlap among the three circles can shift over time without one's job becoming one's life, and without one's call to ministry becoming utterly conflated with work for pay.

Another possibility for envisioning the interplay within a ministerial identity is suggested in Figure 1.2, which depicts God as the all-in-all, with living out one's faith taking the shape of nested dolls. God is not at the center but is holding the whole together.

Mental models for ministry, such as those outlined here, justify the necessity of ministerial leadership development not just for clergy, nor even just for lay leaders in churches, but for all who seek to live out the Christian faith. Whether a person's mental model connecting

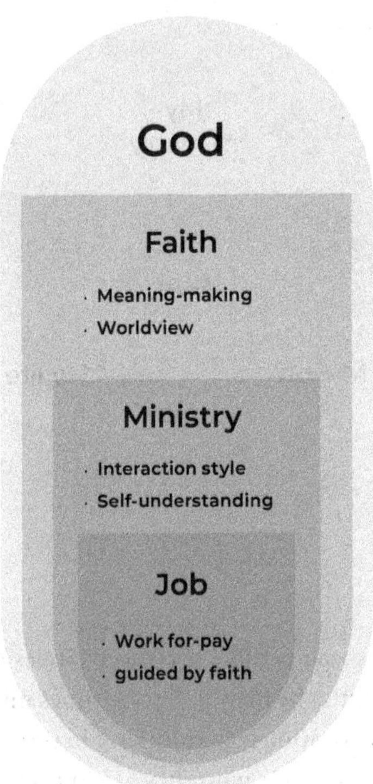

Figure 1.2.

their faith, ministries, and job is clear and straightforward or full of competing commitments and tough decisions, certain principles apply to both figures and suggest numerous other possibilities.

Underlying each figure is an understanding that ministry involves internal cognitive interplay. The minister's leadership begins with an inner life grounded in God and faith in God, and moves outward into relationships and life in the community. Because God and faith are infused with mystery and unknowing—for only God is God—ministerial leadership can only go so far in claiming certainty or defining truth. Ministerial leaders doubt themselves and whether they are doing the right thing not out of insecurity, but as a theological statement of what it means to be human and not God. That doubt finds its counterweight in reliance on the Holy Spirit's presence, movement, and power. Ministerial leadership emerges from within, whether amid a person's work for pay or in their life in family or community. It is not tethered to a particular function. Recognition that ministerial identity transcends a job is key to finding satisfaction in ministry.

Ministerial leadership is not a task but a mentality; it constitutes a way of being a leader. It centers the leader's decision-making on ways of knowing rooted in the Gospel and responsive to the Holy Spirit. It draws out of others in the community the same impulses to follow God's call. Ministers encourage those in their care and all around them to ground their thoughts and actions in what Jesus taught God wants from humanity. A key dimension of ministerial leadership is to motivate those in the minister's care to live out their own ministries. Therefore, ministerial leadership is double-valent: The minister's self and those in the minister's care are intertwined in pursuing the not-fully-knowable will of God.

Ministerial leadership takes place on two levels that interweave with each other. On the first layer, the leader must seek out God's voice through prayer, scripture, tradition, and the teachings of prior life experiences. On the second layer, rather than seeking to persuade those in their care to follow the minister's interpretation, ministerial leaders equip and encourage people to listen for the voice of God in their own lives.

The first layer—where leaders seek out God's will—suggests that the ministerial leader's individual discernment of what is best for the community is important. However, the nature of a not-fully-knowable God insists, however, on an open mind. The leader must trust that God is making God's will known to others, not just themselves, and their effective leadership depends on bringing together the accrued wisdom of the whole, with a curatorial, discriminating mind. Ministerial leaders must carry out God's will as they feel called while recognizing and respecting that everyone else is called in one way or another, too. Therefore, the second layer—where the minister equips others to engage in discernment—is important not just to those in the minister's care, but to the whole community. God might work through anyone, or through any community.

Ministerial leadership thus requires submission to God's will and humility in the face of the reality that God works in the lives of everyone—not just ministers and not just the most faithfully observant. It also requires diplomacy and patience, as interpretations of God's will are bound to differ, and the work of bringing together those who disagree is becoming more difficult in our culture of fractious debate. These two layers—the ministerial leader's discernment of God's will and the discernment of the community—suggest a dialectic that shapes the interchange between the minister and the minister's community. The minister shares a vision, and it changes the people; the people receive the vision, and it changes them, producing a new vision that the minister must then receive, thus becoming changed in turn. This dialectic embodies the very nature of the living word of God.

Effective communal leaders across sectors and settings exchange ideas with their constituents and stakeholders, and all such interchanges generate new ideas and directions. The commonalities between secular and sacred leadership are numerous and varied. All professionals have goals: produce this, fix that, heal the wound, feed the body. Almost all people work to support themselves and their dependents. If they are fortunate, they also work for the sake self-actualization, living out their gifts and values through their jobs, including their jobs' service to others.

Religious leadership is a sector of the economy. Although not all ministerial leaders are paid for their work, their societal roles are comparable to those in law and government, commerce and finance, education, and healthcare. Those fields, too, include different pay structures. Lawyers might be paid handsomely, but volunteer lobbyists and activists occupy the same sector. The teacher in a public school is an educator, as is the Big Brothers/Big Sisters volunteer, as is the home-school parent.

Not one profession within one of those sectors is the same today as it was two generations ago. If anything, ministerial leaders' work is more constant, rather than less so, compared to other professions. That said, changes in other sectors affect ministerial leadership dramatically, altering expectations and rewriting rules of engagement.

Ministry diverges from other forms of work at the point where discernment takes place in relation to goals. A minister's goals do not originate from their own minds, no matter how brilliant; from their boards of directors, no matter how demanding; or from their clients, no matter how expectant. The ministerial leader sets goals that align with what they understand to be God's vision for the world. The minister discerns the right goals to pursue with the help of the Holy Spirit, the ephemeral messenger God sent among creation to guide the Christian movement.

The ministerial leader's goals originate from their humble interpretation of the action of God's guiding hand, the Christian tradition's teachings, and discussion with others relying on the same sources. The secular leader's goals come from what the leader and the community believe to be the right thing to do. Of course, these two forms of goal setting are largely the same, especially when viewed from the outside. Most persons of faith would likely claim that what they deem "the right thing to do," and what is the will of the Holy Spirit, are inseparable, or at least aligned.

Ministry work is, therefore, part of the unending (at least at this point, until Jesus's return or history's end) project of causing the world to look as God intends it to be. Fourth- and fifth-century Christian theologian Augustine of Hippo described God's realm as "the city of God,"[1] which coexists with the material world, but in a different dimension. When a person engages in ministry, that person plays a part, big or small, in building the city of God. The work of the Christian is to imagine the city of God, in partnership with community, and make this world look more like it. Do other leaders make communities better? Of course they do. And if they rely on a higher power in discerning goals, they could rightly be called ministers carrying out their ministerial leadership.

Ministers engage in the double-valent action described above: The ministerial leader makes choices based on their sense of the movement of the Holy Spirit. They set goals for their institutions the same way. At the same time, they encourage and equip those in their care—parishioners, students, patients—to engage in their own interpretations of the Spirit's movement.

As leaders encourage communities to listen for God's voice, their interpretation of a good direction for the community comes into contact with the faithful interpretations of those who receive their ministry. Leaders must respect and respond to the community members' callings. They must also think and act scrupulously when their visions clash with those of their community members, never confusing any one person's interpretations with God's pure, unknowable will. Sharing and comparing interpretations of the Spirit's leading calls for a dance among visions.

Leadership that is not ministerial in nature has a definition of success embedded in it that is comparatively easy to describe. A company can be successful even if it enacts the will of a CEO without regard for a higher power's will. As long as that CEO leads the organization toward a positive bottom line—whatever the bottom line might be—the origin of goals is uncomplicated by supernatural forces. Discernment toward goals of this earth, not reliant on messages coming to human beings from a heavenly realm, requires more walking, less dancing.

An executive is likely to be more successful if they take feedback seriously, but ultimately, they will only be rewarded for doing so if the results are good. Executives in fields from law to higher education may find that good things happen when all views are invited into dialogue, but the practice of engaging the community is not core to the mission of the organization. Dialogue sometimes results in a new direction, but its more typical benefits are side-effects, like high morale and staff retention.

Leadership in fields other than ministry relies on tangible forms of reason, such as numbers ("Are we making money?"), popular aesthetics ("Do people find our work attractive and want to consume it?"), and correctness vis-à-vis the body politic ("Is this legal?"). Ministerial leadership, by contrast, follows the movement of the Spirit, which can be sensed but not defined and which is in constant motion.

Ordained, Christian, ministerial leaders have the capacity to convene conversations about the Spirit's movement and coordinate a response to multiple reactions to its guidance, but they do not access a special frequency unavailable to others, including those they are charged to lead. Of course, this assertion stems from a particular interpretation of ordination not shared by all Christian traditions, making it all the more important to name the specific cosmology from which this assumption emerges.

God's realm is all around us, existing in a parallel universe to the earth rather than "above" as Figure 1.3 suggests in its two-dimensional imperfection. Yet the main point of the figure must be stated, despite the faulty dimensionality: Jesus is the only being occupying the space in-between God and creation in any sustained way. Humans intercede, and God breaks in through human activities in the busy space between heaven and earth. But no human, including clergy, can say, "I *live* in that in-between space."

Does this mean that ordination is not important and that clergy should have no special role or say in faith community leadership? Yes and no. If *special* means "special in the eyes of God," then no: Clergy are not any more important to God than any other created being. God's love for creation is so far beyond what human beings can understand that seeking to parse proportions is a futile exercise. If "special" means

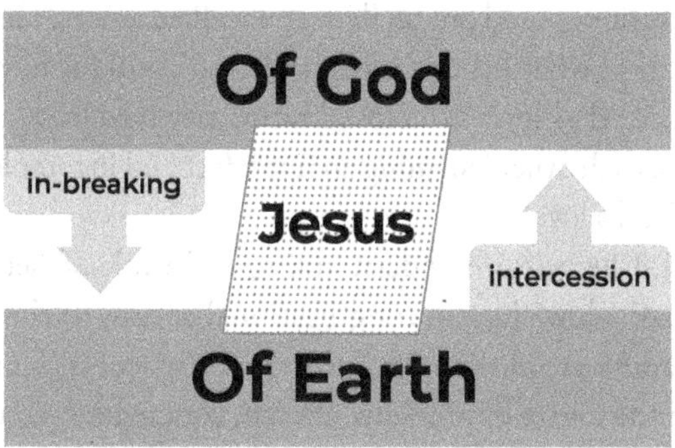

Figure 1.3.

possessing gifts, training, and focus that earn respect and merit the delegation of authority, then clergy are special indeed.

Furthermore, even in a culture where religious leadership is just as likely to be considered suspicious as valuable, people trust ministers. They assume ministers have special access to something that is of God, and they believe ministers' words about religion, God, and the best way to live life. Despite a steady stream of news about ministerial misconduct, ministers receive unusual levels of confidence, and their bad actions elicit intense disappointment. In their disappointment, people call the minister a hypocrite, but that label only makes sense for one presumed to be accountable to a high standard. Ministers do not have special "God phones" connecting them to the divine, but they have special gifts and set-apart responsibilities. Communities trust that ministers embody goodness and know how to lead. This unspoken trust becomes evident when communities express horror at having their expectations disappointed.

What role does Jesus play in the cosmology described here? As stated, only Jesus occupies the mysterious space between heaven and earth as a permanent resident. The rest of humanity has fleeting forays into that space but cannot, in this life, occupy or know it fully. Jesus came into creation to demonstrate how God wanted humanity to live. God had tried to reach God's children again and again, persuading them to discern God's will and to follow it, but ultimately—possibly out of sheer exasperation—God put on flesh and walked among God's people. Jesus taught that what lies at the heart of God's will for humanity can best be described as love. God loved humanity into being and wants people to love each other, pursuing an imperfect and incomplete approximation of God's love.

Figure 1.3 suggests an understanding of the role of clergy in what one might call a low church, congregationalist way, in that ordained religious leaders are absent from the center space; in fact, they are absent from the entire figure. Low-church, congregational ordination is understood to set a person apart from the rest without moving them beyond the realm of the human. Whether a person is called to ministry is a matter of individual and communal interpretation that includes mystical and practical dimensions. Ordination is important but does not elevate a person to another plane of reality.

This low-church, congregationalist understanding has wider implications regarding leadership development than just the matter of who is and is not ordained. It implies that hierarchies in organizations should be flat, as God favors no one. Role designation and clarification replace top-down organizational structures. Roles in such a structure hinge on gifts, training, and the needs of the community. They are about efficiency in achieving a mission, not God's favor.

In communities where the ordained are set apart but not elevated, leadership can and should be shared across constituents to maximize good ideas and harness all available energies toward the cause. Leaders and their constituents share a context, and that context matters greatly. Contexts differ from one another. They are specific, and worthy of special—even unique—consideration. From the earliest days of the church, it has been clear that what works in one setting is not necessarily supposed to work everywhere. Hierarchies foster efficiency—nothing more and nothing less. Relationships of mutual regard and loving care are inherently good and serve as the connective tissue that holds communities together—not a charismatic (cult) leader, and not fear.

Many organizations embody the values of shared leadership, where roles differentiate people without implying any metaphysical elevation over one another. What makes the Christian community special is not its ordained leader; it is Jesus. The Christian faith community specifically calls followers of Jesus to partner with each other in the pursuit of a world that is more loving and reflective of God's intentions for creation.

Not all religious leaders understand their roles as ones where they are leading from within a community. Although the study of ministerial leadership development might not be entirely tradition-specific, religious leaders understand their roles differently across and within faith traditions. To say that all leaders' motivations are basically the same would be arrogant and insensitive to religious diversity. For instance, many Christians would balk at the idea that all of them have a ministry;

the "ministry of all believers" is a distinctly Protestant concept that not even all Protestants embrace. Jewish religious leaders, by contrast, do not refer to themselves as ministers.

Furthermore, many nonreligious leaders do believe themselves to lead from within a community and toward a shared mission. In an America where division is the norm and collaboration the exception, leaders who are able to bring people together around a common cause are both rare and increasingly sought after. Town library directors and school superintendents face challenges that require them to develop leaders around them who can help them build consensus and protect institutions from partisan division. Many organizations embrace a definition of leadership in which the leader is part of the community, and this work calls more and more upon leaders to empower those around them to help them face the headwinds of dramatic and rapid cultural change. Religious leadership might differ from other forms because of its orientation toward the divine, but the charisms of a communal leader vary within the category of religious leadership and have counterparts in secular, mission-driven work.

To craft a definition of ministerial leadership, one begins with a distinctive sort of goal that is ephemeral, intangible, and spiritual. The goal has mystical but not altogether mysterious dimensions, as it might be as God-given as it is commonsensical. Many non-Christians work toward goals that are not about money or concrete, measurable attainments, such as educators who teach for transformation and artists who render into the material world that which comes from beyond it.

The great challenge of ministerial leadership—defined as communal leadership guided by the Holy Spirit and requiring that leaders honor and draw out the Spirit's work in everyone in the leader's care—is the challenge of ever feeling like one is doing it right or even well. Because their bottom line is not easily or quickly definable, ministerial leaders never feel like their work is sufficient. This sense of never-enough-ness causes leaders to treat the art and science of leadership as something beyond human ken, rather than as an area for intentional learning and growth. Whereas God might be beyond our capacity for full understanding, leadership is not. Just because ministerial leadership includes mystical dimensions that place its results beyond human control does not mean that one's practice of it cannot be improved. Just because it is difficult to lead well does not mean leaders cannot grow in their mastery of the task. Given the demands that press in on them, they must address the need for lifelong learning intentionally. They must start somewhere.

Whether out of sheer overwhelm, or a belief that it will not make a difference, ministerial leaders in the Christian tradition rarely devote even a fraction of the time needed to develop themselves as leaders. In their preparation through theological education, they likely received messages that leadership was not important to the role of faith leader, so even if they took a course or two that introduced them to leadership theory, the absence of options for leadership learning shaped their attitudes.

Ministerial leaders today serve amid expectations that are both seemingly impossible to meet and rapidly changing. Reports of overwhelm make rational sense, considering that practices of continuing education for ministerial leadership occupy a negligibly small place among a vast array of responsibilities. As unprecedented as today's challenges might be, professional development neglect is a primary culprit in perpetuating a sense among ministerial leaders that they are not ready and not equipped to guide the church or any other mission-driven community through these tumultuous times in human history.

Current Ministerial Leadership Development Models and Their Insufficiency

A common statement one hears about leadership today is, "The old ways don't work anymore." Any assertion that suggests a longing for the "good old days" should give pause. In the past, those in positions of power found life easier because unchecked oppression was often a side-effect of the privilege that came with leadership. Communities were less diverse, and in communities that happened to be diverse, there was no question as to who would make decisions: the historically advantaged. Realistically, there were no "old ways" of cultivating and sustaining good practices for ministerial leadership. There was never a time when it was taught adequately well. The good news is that this void makes room to build new practices attuned to contemporary times.

The Era in Which Ministerial Leaders Lead

Before unpacking the assertion that ministerial leadership education has had no "golden age"—at least not yet—some background regarding cultural history is important. Leadership happens in a context. When anyone harkens back to a season when ministerial leadership was easier, they are likely pointing to a period in the intellectual history of Europe and North America known now as the modern era, loosely defined as spanning from the early nineteenth century to the 1970s.

Beginning with the Enlightenment, when post-Renaissance thinkers began to explore the communal implications of humanity's immense potential to control nature, institutions of all kinds began to flourish. The contours of the underlying assumptions about life's purpose and meaning during the modern era include characteristics such as these: Human beings can achieve anything to which they set their minds, a singular set of rules governs all human activities, and the nature of truth is singular. Leaders control the pace and shape of change. They also control interactions among communities under their authority.

One can see in these contours of the modern era how institutions and their leaders might have found those times to be a straightforward—if not easy—period. If human beings expect that they can conquer the universe, believe in rule-following, and assume that leaders are in charge of everything, then leaders are virtually unchecked in their authority. Leadership development could focus exclusively on skills; the culture did the rest. Time management? Nine to five. Change in leadership? What "change"?

The 1960s were a watershed era in the United States and elsewhere in the world as the assumptions of the modern era gave way to the postmodern era. The belief that human beings could achieve anything became a frightening premise in the nuclear age, and the war in Vietnam raised many questions as to whether leaders should have unchecked power. Science showed its vulnerabilities when it was unable to answer significant questions such as when life begins or whether might makes right on the battlefield.

Understandings of truth proliferated—became multiple—as many different communities sought a voice during the women's and civil rights movements. Different definitions of the nature of life had to find a way into dialogue with one another. Leaders, from parents to presidents, no longer controlled interactions between communities, as technologies emerged that defied knowledge centralization.

Further complexity arose in the form of intersectional identities, not just within neighborhoods, but within individuals. No longer could the wider society categorize a whole city, neighborhood, family, or individual into tidy boxes. Self-actualization led people to realize that they were even more different from one another than they had initially thought, and they became less willing to be placed into categories for the sake of others' efficiency.

No longer does a single subset of a single community—white men—corner the market on executive leadership, although reversion to such assumptions continues to this day and intensifies amidst generalized, communal anxiety about rapid change. Leaders began to rise to power who came from different backgrounds, but at the same time, leaders came under new scrutiny. The ranks of leadership became more diverse just as reflexive trust in leaders began to unravel.

The postmodern era gave way in the early twenty-first century. The jury is out among intellectual theorists and historians about what happened, and what is happening, in this new era. If one were to consider the modern era as a time when culture was tightly controlled by monolithic definitions of truth and leadership, and the postmodern era as a time when that invisible but ironclad control over culture fragmented into multiple modes of meaning-making, then the first phase of what followed postmodernism might be described as "new tribalism." As a response to postmodernity's fragmentation—where truth's multiplicity made everything from peaceful civic discourse to collaborative elementary school curriculum development nearly impossible—communities came back together, but in new and localized ways.

New tribalism describes a specific kind of factionalism, where communities find like-minded counterparts with whom they define truth together, internally. Many resist the term "tribal," with its pejorative connotations and risk of slighting native cultures. The good news is that the era is likely already over without a name ever having settled in. New tribalism rose and fell quickly because monolithic definitions of truth are hard to hold together. Multiple monoliths, constantly exposed to the ideas of others, tumbled like so many towers of Babel, though construction continues as new tribalism gives way.

Gives way, however, to what? If the years between 9/11 and COVID-19 were ones where tribes consolidated, post-COVID communities are coalescing differently and confusingly. New tribalism might define certain dimensions of politics, but although small pockets of populations wall themselves off from each other, those walls are by necessity porous. Even violent subcultures that coordinated an attack on the US Capitol on January 6, 2021, have come under intense scrutiny by the larger whole. The human tendency to seek out "their people" has tremendous promise for community-building, but when that tendency goes wrong, it can go very wrong. It can also go very right, and leaders are wise to pay attention to the communal impulse to band together, harnessing it into new energy.

What possibilities arise as communities gather in new, sometimes frightening and sometimes exciting, ways? Where is the culture today with regard to how communities coalesce and understand themselves? A contender for describing the present moment is to call it an era of "emergence." *Emergence* describes an entity that is unformed but taking shape. In its incompleteness, emergence is challenging to describe, but that uncertainty is part of what defines a period of emergence.

Cultural theorists who write about emergence provide guidance for defining and leading the community in this burgeoning era.

Community organizer and scholar adrienne maree brown describes these times as ones in which leaders must shift away from control and toward creativity.[2] In other words, modernism's obsession with control and postmodernity's determination to undermine control are equally useless when leaders seek pathways ahead. Brown argues in favor of multiple perspectives on truth, beauty, reason, and power. Leaders can and must take into consideration all forms of knowing regarding human motivations.

Brown is no anarchist. She writes that the notion that institutional control is the enemy of social change is, if nothing else, outdated. "We try to leverage control over the natural world by making our emotions and sensations less reliable than our thoughts, and then burn at the stake anyone who stays attuned to the ways of power and pleasure in the natural world. It's counterproductive."[3] The concepts presented in her book, *Emergent Strategy: Shaping Change in a Changing World*, include a conviction that hierarchies are acceptable if they foster efficiency and role clarity. She writes that leading from love is better than leading from outrage. Her writing suggests that attunement to power dynamics indicates responsible leadership, not collusion, for power is not inherently evil; it just *is*. Guilt does not energize, and going with what feels good is often right. Cultivating happiness results in alignment between leaders' actions and the best path.

In developing her theories of emergent leadership, brown relies on metaphors from the natural world beyond human beings (who are, of course, also part of nature). She points to mushrooms' underground interconnectedness, ant colonies' cooperation, ferns' completeness even when they are tiny, starlings' synchronicity, and dandelions' resilience. She describes recent scientific compromise on the nature of light: It is both a wave *and* a particle. Both are true at the same time, despite centuries-long debate among scholars insisting it was one or the other.

In an emergent season, leaders must rely on emotions, for what is happening around them is not knowable in fully rational ways today. Perhaps "reality" was never fully knowable, but for generations, leaders were expected to define it. Control becomes less important, and attunement more important, in emergent leadership. Cultivation of psychological synchronicity with constituents supersedes persuasion as a key leadership practice.

Difficulty in relinquishing (illusions of) control is more difficult for some than others. In his book *Beyond Whiteness: An Education in Belonging*, Willie James Jennings writes that values for possession, control, and mastery are so interwoven with white supremacy that white supremacy cannot be dismantled without a referendum on those values.[4] Conversely, those who never had very much power will not find shifting from control to attunement as difficult. People who have been conventionally kept out of the corridors of power have less to lose than those who tacitly understood themselves as expected to rule the world.

In her book, *How to Lead When You Don't Know Where You Are Going: Leading in a Liminal Season*,[5] Susan Beaumont provides definitions of emergence that take into account its mysteriousness. She distinguishes between a process that emerges and a process that is tightly controlled. The former is characterized by experimentation and its related risks. The latter is characterized by high stakes and fear of failure.[6] Beaumont writes that the current leadership season is an in-between time with precedent in the history of Christianity. Moses led those who wandered through the wilderness for more than a generation. The disciples of Jesus fretted over what to do until Jesus returned. How does one bring a community together and mobilize them toward lofty aims when they are looking to the horizon, waiting? Moses and Aaron, Jesus's disciples, and the Apostle Paul provide insights into the leadership challenge of waiting while watching for signs of what is to come.

Leaders face two tempting shortcuts around the difficult work liminality requires, according to Beaumont. On the one hand, they are tempted to fall back on old ways to make everyone feel safe. On the other hand, they wish to rush to closure to manage their own anxiety and that of others, pretending to have all the answers.[7] Beaumont argues that emergent leaders must do what it takes to stay in the moment, for God is doing—gestating—something new.

But how does one stay attentive, rather than reactive, when a community is looking to its leader to resolve its disorientation and take it somewhere—anywhere—beyond uncertainty? Beaumont writes that leaders must sustain enough busyness to reduce anxiety about whether the leader can be trusted to perform their duties.[8] Communities invest confidence in leaders who maintain a rigorous schedule and portfolio of responsibilities, and leaders need the buy-in that communal confidence affords them. Leaders must sustain the status quo while simultaneously agitating against it, preventing the backsliding that is the inevitable result of attempting to stand still in a shifting tide. Leaders in a season of emergence must support innovation while also nurturing coherence, allowing the cultural pregnancy of this in-between moment to take its course.

During a season of emergence, leaders must deploy or withhold patience, depending on whether urgent action or waiting for more clarity is necessary. Leaders must constantly broaden their horizons, as new inputs come at them from every direction. They must advocate for those in their care to broaden their horizons too, so that the community might feel adequately safe, but not too comfortable. Leadership development in an era of emergence has the ultimate goal of forming mature leaders. What are the marks of maturity to which leaders should aspire? Acceptance that more than one thing can be true at the same time; self-knowledge and attunement to the needs of the community; patience in some situations and impatience in others, depending on whether urgency or attentiveness is called for; and, finally, acceptance of the answer, "It depends."

Letting go of an unhealthy need for control is a process, not an event. The parent of the education-for-liberation movement, Paulo Freire, wrote that both oppressors and those they oppress are playing roles.[9] Each fears the loss that might result from being released from those roles, so consciousness-raising feels risky for each, though for different reasons. The cost of failing to grow in consciousness is higher, however. The oppressed person who does not become liberated from their self-perceived roles is likely to define success using the definitions around them, becoming an oppressor at the first opportunity rather than redefining reality. Emergent leadership comes with loss in letting go as well as freedom from constraints built on obsolete expectations for communal leaders.

The Null Curriculum

Leaders require guidance on what forms of lifelong learning will enable them to lead in this day and age. The overview of periods of intellectual history offered above lands human communities in the era of emergence. Naturally, one might assume that the present days call for a new way because the old ways are not working anymore. In fact, when it comes to leadership development, there are no "old ways" that one could call sustained, sequenced, intentional approaches to leadership development. Much of past practice for ministerial leadership development, usually not even called "leadership development," came to learners through what is known as a null curriculum.

A tacit or implicit curriculum, in the world of education theory, describes a way in which a student learns through osmosis based on atmosphere and environment. They take their cues about how to lead from how leaders behave, and how constituent followers react to them. Learning leadership through a tacit curriculum calls on students to mimic effective leaders and sort out what does and does not work for them. Some internalize leadership skills well, adopting best practices and understanding the worst practices as helpful examples of what not to do. Others simply adopt behaviors without considering whether those behaviors are authentic to them, or right for the community, blindly accepting best and worst practices as the done thing.

A null curriculum refers to the way in which lacunae in curricula signal to students what is or is not important. What is not taught, discussed, or even mentioned bespeaks unimportance. With the possible exceptions of schools of business and public policy, most professionals' thinking about leadership is influenced more by a null curriculum than a tacit or formal curriculum. The absence of required courses[10] on how to guide an institution for those who will be tasked with doing just that says, "You will learn leadership through trial-and-error," or, "You will learn leadership on-the-job," or, "Any idiot could figure out how to be a good leader."

Doctors and lawyers take few or no courses on leadership theory, even though they are likely to guide institutions and supervise people. Most of their learning comes to them on-the-job, through observation and trial-and-error. Seminary education is no different. The absence of education for leadership development sends the message that the students need not receive formal training, but rather they should and must learn it elsewhere. Consider this brief history of leadership education at a particular institution of theological higher education, the one served by this book's author: Andover Newton Seminary at Yale Divinity School.

The most commonly shared story of the birth of this oldest graduate school of any kind in the United States focuses on a theological dispute. A breakaway faction of faculty members left Harvard during the Unitarian Controversy. Henry Ware, a Unitarian, was elected to the Hollis Chair at Harvard. Fearing a departure from orthodoxy, two professors started a new school. One of those two faculty members was married to a member of the Phillips family, which was starting a school in Andover, Massachusetts, so the faction moved there and started Andover Seminary, a postcollegiate theological school and the first graduate school of any kind in the US.

What is less well known about Andover's founding was that, amid the Second Great Awakening, appreciation was on the rise for clergy who were both spiritually on fire and intellectually grounded. Timothy Dwight, who was serving as Yale's president at the time, delivered the opening convocation address during Andover's inaugural year and warned against the "quackery" that could result from inadequately trained ministers. Was he saying that Harvard was teaching quacks? No, nor was he addressing Harvard's theological shift. Instead, he was referring to those whose theological education came primarily through what we would now call "apprenticeships," often pursued after college—or even without completing college. Going to Harvard and Yale was not a typical pathway into pastoral ministry in the early nineteenth century. In those days, Yale and Harvard were small schools that served only those whose wealthy families were able to spare the labor on their farms. More often, young men would be identified in local communities as having gifts for ministry. It was in those communities where they would become educated for ministry.

Those young men would go to work assisting pastors—their own or those in neighboring towns—move into the pastor's parsonage to gain access to his library, serve alongside him, and eventually succeed him. This form of education was effective when the minister was effective, and not so effective when the minister was not. But even those who trained under the best—including the protégées of Timothy Dwight's grandfather, Jonathan Edwards—were bound to have a narrow point of view.

Dwight argued that ministry was simply too important to leave to informal education. In addition to providing postcollegiate learning, graduate theological schools removed apprentices from parsonages and pulled candidates for ministry together under the guidance of theological faculty members. This move was good for students' intellectual development and offered seminarians the kind of learning found among peers: iron sharpening iron. What got lost from the very beginning, however, was the leadership development young men (and, at the time, only men were eligible for theological education) found in apprenticeships, where they tried, failed, and tried again. Despite the occasional quackery, good things surely had happened in apprenticeships, as candidates for ministry grew in their readiness to lead by expanding their repertoires, reflecting on their choices, and gaining important skills.

Beneficial as faculty instruction and peer learning were, Andover Newton has been trying to correct for the mistake of removing theological education from the realm of practice since 1807. Education for a profession, particularly a quickly changing profession, must align closely with the profession itself. Otherwise, how does the educator protect the curriculum from obsolescence? How can the student learn to learn in the face of previously unimaginable challenges if not by engaging with theology in the most hand-on ways possible? A blended education that includes both experience and classroom learning would have been a better alternative then, and it remains a better alternative now.

Yale and Harvard created graduate schools of theology not long after Andover's founding, and then the Baptists decided to get into the game. The First Baptist Church of Boston decided to establish a seminary of its own in 1825 that it would build in the far hinterlands outside Boston, now the toniest of suburbs: Newton, Massachusetts. Its purpose was to educate Baptist clergy, whereas Andover served Congregationalists in those earliest days of denominational separation in the US. Newton's first faculty members were, however, Andover graduates. Both Andover and Newton had good years and bad years, successful and unsuccessful leaders, and through a series of incidents and accidents they came together in the 1930s, first as co-inhabitants of the Newton campus, and later as a merged entity. To its credit, the school never forgot that it was founded to provide the church with a learned clergy. Of course, "church" and "clergy" are both terms that mean something somewhat different now than they did in the school's early days. That said, the school, to this day, understands whom it serves.

It got out of the apprenticeship business for far too long, but it also came back to it earlier than its peers. In the 1950s, the faculty of Andover Newton began to rediscover its responsibilities to form not just theologians but also ministerial leaders capable of serving and guiding communities. A particular dean—later president—George Peck created a "Church and Ministry Department" meant to serve as an elbow joint between the theological academy and local congregations. Most notable in the school's reclamation of its commitment to developing pastoral leaders was its founding of the nation's first accredited supervised ministry program.

As the story goes, many students in the 1960s found jobs in local churches as youth program directors, and on Sunday afternoons, they would get together on the basketball court to shoot hoops and chew fat. Some faculty members stepped onto the court to join in the game and overheard students' conversations about how they were connecting their classroom learning with the life of the church through their part-time jobs. The faculty decided to get intentional about this style of experiential learning followed by theological reflection, and thus the Field Education Program was born.

Around the same time, Andover Newton's faculty was exploring the emerging field of psychology and religion, and interning chaplains serving in hospital settings—most notably mental healthcare hospitals—needed sophisticated supervision over their ministries that required both expert and peer support. Clinical Pastoral Education (CPE), has since evolved into the gold standard for formation in pastoral care. Through it, students serve as interns in high-intensity settings where pastoral needs, whether acute or chronic, are existentially challenging. Through one-on-one counsel with expert supervisors, group reflection, and skills-based learning, a student's time in CPE is divided evenly between working as a chaplain and reflecting on that work, thereby deepening capacities for guiding those in the minister's care toward a more life-giving perspective on crises and suffering.

Even with these pioneering moves, Andover Newton's faculty did not dedicate significant time to instruction in ministerial leadership. Most teaching for leadership was entrusted to supervised ministry, where those providing the supervision were themselves inadequately educated for leadership. Beyond an internship, a course here and there, and prior experience or schooling, no graduate of a theological seminary has dedicated significant attention to leadership development over the past two hundred-plus years, especially given the intense demands of ministerial leadership today. Even the pre-Andover apprenticeship model was deeply flawed. Whereas it could have been reformed, it was discarded—like the proverbial baby thrown out with the bathwater—as the modern era dawned and ministers trusted that rational learning would suffice to prepare a pastor for anything.

Graduate Theological Education for Ministry

Ministers learn their trade in numerous ways—formal, informal, and cultural. Today, graduate theological education is the primary pathway to ministry as a profession in most Christian traditions, even though such education varies in formality from church-based Bible schools to Ivy League advanced degrees. Learning for leadership has never been a central emphasis in these settings, and considering the leadership challenges of ministry, one wonders why. Understandable explanations are readily available.

First, graduate professional education for ministry—"theological education"—emphasizes foundational teachings in theology. That it is even called "theological education" rather than "education for ministerial leadership" suggests as much. Today, a master of divinity degree must include the following component parts to pass muster for accreditation, which is necessary for courses to be transferable and for seminary students to be eligible for federal financial aid:

> (a) [R]eligious heritage, including understanding of scripture, the theological traditions and history of the school's faith community, and the broader heritage of other relevant religious traditions; (b) cultural context, including attention to cultural and social issues, to global awareness and engagement, and to the multifaith and multicultural nature of the societies in which students may serve; (c) personal and spiritual formation, including development in personal faith, professional ethics, emotional maturity, moral integrity, and spirituality; and (d) religious and public leadership, including cultivating capacities for leading in ecclesial or denominational and public contexts and reflecting on leadership practices.[11]

Leadership receives only passing mention in the fourth and final area of study expected for a master of divinity. This near-omission results from the fact that leadership, as an area of scholarly inquiry, is far younger than theological education—the first form of graduate education in the United States. Business schools came into existence in the twentieth century, and the study of leadership in other fields is younger still. Yet the assumption that leadership can be learned after seminary, during a first call in a congregation, is embedded in these accreditation standards.

Practical ministry education has long included instruction on preaching and pastoral care, but neither of those fields has fared well amid a hierarchy of disciplines that places the most abstract of fields, such as those that rely on multiple ancient languages, at the highest level.[12] In the rarefied air of academia, scholars of more abstract topics are deemed the truly smart. Those who grapple with areas of inquiry that include people, communities, and life's messiness fall further down the food chain. This is similar to what happens in college classics departments, which might have only one or two students but great influence in faculty politics. Similarly, those who teach in practical areas at times find themselves tacitly relegated to the kids' table in intellectual debates within theological faculties, trotted out to offer devotions or to respond to crises deemed pastoral.

In other words, "practical" translates as "optional" in the deep culture of theological education, despite the great contributions of practical theologians over the past century. Therefore, introducing yet another practical concern—leadership—involves a twofold challenge. First, attention to it requires the insertion of yet another discipline into an already overcrowded curriculum. Second, that same overcrowding threatens those who focus on more abstract disciplines, who fear losing pride of place, accustomed as they are to being in charge.[13]

Ironically, the few who teach ministerial leadership in graduate theological schools tend to advocate strongly for classical theological learning. If today's ministers cannot tend the fire of the Christian tradition, all will be lost in the next generation. Generally, scholars of ministerial leadership appreciate that seminary graduates must, first and foremost, know and convey the stories that make the Christian faith what it is. Their primary obligation is to make spiritual sense of the world around them so that those in their care can do the same.[14]

Multiple options exist for leadership learning that stretch far beyond the classroom, which cannot necessarily be said for theology and Bible study. What proponents of leadership education in theological schools seek is attention to leadership that provides preparation to move from theology to practice, to terrains beyond our current knowing. Educators must understand that leadership needs to be learned, rather than simply gleaned, especially in the dawning era. Protecting the Christian tradition will require not just knowledge, but healthy communities to tend that knowledge—and healthy communities require good leaders. Teaching leadership is not the same as teaching content-oriented disciplines, however. It involves creating neural pathways between theology and action in the community.

The academy has presented one form of resistance to leadership learning for ministers by centering and privileging more abstract concepts. North American culture simultaneously put up another wall in the mid-twentieth century, placing ministers outside the realm of cultural leadership, assuming them to be the chaplains to the "real" leaders in communities, such as politicians and businessmen. Successful ministers were strong preachers but otherwise the Casper Milquetoasts of high society, heard from only rarely, and certainly never rocking the boat.

On the one hand, the assumption that ministers are not *real* cultural leaders, beyond the confines of the church, has some grounding in theology. Jesus Christ is the true head of the church, and clerical demagoguery has caused nothing but harm in Western history. Jesus stated plainly and unambiguously that no earthly leader would sit at his right or left hand, but that the community would share leadership based on their faith and their gifts. The true follower of Jesus would be a servant, not one who would be served. Consider this account of Jesus's ministry:

> Then the mother of the sons of Zebedee came to him with her sons, and kneeling before him, she asked a favor of him. And he said to her, "What do you want?" She said to him, "Declare that these two sons of mine will sit, one at your right hand and one at your left, in your kingdom." But Jesus answered, "You do not know what you are asking. Are you able to drink the cup that I am about to drink?" They said to him, "We are able." He said to them, "You will indeed drink my cup, but to sit at my

> right hand and at my left, this is not mine to grant, but it is for those for whom it has been prepared by my Father."
>
> When the ten heard it, they were angry with the two brothers. But Jesus called them to him and said, "You know that the rulers of the Gentiles lord it over them, and their great ones are tyrants over them. It will not be so among you; but whoever wishes to be great among you must be your servant, and whoever wishes to be first among you must be your slave; just as the Son of Man came not to be served but to serve, and to give his life a ransom for many."
>
> —Matthew 20:20–28

The Christian movement was avowedly separate from the corridors of political power, rendering unto Caesar that which was Caesar's (Matthew 22:21) and otherwise quietly undermining imperial control from house-church dinner tables. All changed when Roman Emperor Constantine converted to Christianity in the fourth century CE. The fact that dates were traditionally set using "AD," *anno domini* ("the year of our Lord"), indicates the beginning of time by which dates are now set underlines the ways in which Christianity and power married one another in Rome. The blending of politics and Christianity probably saved the Christian movement from the oblivion suffered by its contemporaries—namely, other religious movements of the time, now deemed either cults or heresies—but it also complicated the relationship between Christian ministry and cultural leadership.

Christian ministers collaborated, consulted, and colluded with political and economic leaders in different ways over the centuries. In the US context, post–World War II modernity represented a time when institutional power swelled to new heights, and those who had power were (mostly Protestant) Christians. White Anglo-Saxon Protestants controlled economic resources, and ministers did not need to work hard to get people to church, given the social ostracism those with economic and political power would suffer were they to sleep in. Furthermore, joining civic organizations was simply what people did, as work—at least for the privileged—was becoming less all-consuming. Participating in civic life outside the workplace signaled prosperity, reminiscent as it was of a leisure class in possession of inherited wealth.

Even during the season of prosperity for institutions in the 1950s, however, the cultural power of the clergy was under threat from forces inside and out. In an article titled "Reclaiming Professional Jurisdiction: The Re-Emergence of the Theological Task of Ministry," Gil Rendle wrote in the early 2000s about a pattern that has only accelerated since, where new professions emerge and infringe on the territory once understood to be the responsibility of the minister.[15] This change does not just press in from beyond congregations, Rendle writes, but also changes dynamics within them. "Experts" in the congregation in matters of finance and human resources undermine the authority of the pastor to lead a staff or make mission-appropriate budget decisions, no longer regarding the pastor as omniscient or omnicompetent within those walls. In turn, encroachment on the traditional jurisdiction of Christian ministers presses in from the outside, as newly developed professions proliferate and take up more and more cultural space.

The counseling role of the minister serves as an example of the complexity resulting from the matrix of professions adjacent to ministry. Ministers at one time served as therapists to individuals and families in their congregations. Even leaders beyond the church's membership rolls sought them out for guidance. Today, ministerial professional guilds insist that pastors refer parishioners with psychological concerns to trained, specialized psychotherapists. Thankfully, many do, because what is known today about mental health today is so much vaster than what was known two or three generations ago; no one professional could carry it all. The change is not a bad thing, but it is a change.

Ministers also functioned as moral arbiters in their communities, intervening and advocating for those experiencing conflict. They were the judges; they were the social workers. As communities become more diverse, and the problems they face more complex, no individual in any single profession can serve every need adequately.

Over-functioning beyond their expertise risks harm to the community and deprives the community of the vast knowledge now available across professional fields.

The public once turned to its faith leaders for help; now, others provide that help, and they often do it better. What do ministerial leaders still have to offer? A great deal. But the areas where they have the most relevant, specific role are the areas where they receive the least training: guiding people in making meaning out of life events and working with individuals to build a sense of community. These two elements of a happy and satisfied life are the obvious terrain of the religious leader, but their training includes little attention to community building and only a bit more to helping others to make meaning. Few in the wider culture would define the importance of ministers in those terms—community building and meaning making—as those benefits of life in a faith community are stated plainly only rarely.

That disconnect between what society needs from religious leaders and what they are prepared to offer harms churches and their viability for the future. The disconnect results in deprivation: Communities need leadership in building community and making spiritual sense of the world around them, yet they do not define their needs using those words or seeking those gifts. Not looking for those gifts in their religious leaders, they do not find them. Then, they look elsewhere to get those needs met rather than demanding that the church and its ministers reform themselves to reestablish relevance.

Today, educated, prosperous people stumble upon a fitness trend that includes meditation, and they feel as though they have discovered a new planet. A hard-core atheist engages in service for needy people in their community who find transformation they believe no one else could understand. Others find themselves desperately lonely and look for love in all the wrong places, chasing dopamine surges rather than real connection. Professional encroachment took certain jurisdictions away from ministerial leaders. Now, a course correction is in order, and it is ministers who will need to do the correcting. Ministers must shift their attention to aiding their communities in meaning making and relationship building, and their churches' memberships and denominational support structures must help them prioritize those societal functions.

The growing number of professions that horn in on ministerial territory is particularly evident when one considers the history of religion in higher education. Harvard and Yale, America's oldest universities, came into existence to provide their regions with a learned clergy. Over time, the fields for which young men studied grew in number. Then, new colleges and universities came into existence that served women and prepared learners for fields other than ministry. The advent of graduate theological education, described earlier, related in part to the way in which undergraduate education came to include many other fields. Early nineteenth-century theologians worried that ministry was too important not to call for even more advanced education than other fields. It could not be equated with the study of other disciplines when it came to cultural importance. Later on, postgraduate education for law, medicine, and business arose, following religion's lead.

In the early days of the oldest universities, the first faculty members were ministers who lived within the campus community alongside students. Over time, as the leadership of universities included fewer clergy, university chaplains became the norm, but this did not happen until the early to mid-twentieth century. Faculty, administration, chaplains: Those roles were all rolled up into the body of the faculty. Over the past three generations, specialization fragmented the faculty. Just as the academy educated for a growing array of professions, new professions emerged within it, such as career advising, student affairs, and, most recently, diversity, equity, and inclusion.

Fragmentation led to marginalization, with religion moving farther and farther out onto the periphery. In the nineteenth century, professors carried a chaplaincy role in colleges and universities. As university faculties began to attend to research over teaching, the role of chaplain was separated away from the professor's teaching function. Then, teaching itself moved down the list of priorities as faculty members' research took precedence. Stock in those serving the needs of students has lost value.

In some settings, chaplains were, in the late twentieth century, understood as advisors to the real leaders, such as faculty members with problems or hopelessly technocratic presidents. In the twenty-first century, a university leader who consulted with the chaplain might be viewed as odd, weak, or superstitious.

Crises in culture and the academy have more recently begun to call on presidents to engage in meaning making and community building. They are expected to speak thoughtfully on questions about diversity within the academy, and the value of higher education to the wider society. Constituents critique presidents harshly if they get statements on tragedies in and beyond their communities wrong. If ministers are ill equipped to engage in the work of building community and guiding others in making spiritual sense, imagine how ill prepared a university president, selected for their fundraising potential first and foremost, would be. They must rethink and reassert their institutions' loftier missions amid widespread doubt about higher education's capacity to transform or even improve a broken world. The notion of the university president and the university chaplain joining forces in the face of these needs would be inspiring were it not so unrealistic. Clergy on campus are already so far out on the fringes that it is hard to envision a path back to the center where they might aid in renewing attention to mission and meaning.

The university's earliest leaders were spiritual leaders. As leadership roles fragmented, research came out on top, and spiritual meaning making fell by the wayside. Now, university leaders disappoint their communities when they fail at spiritual meaning making. This pattern mirrors the role of the church in the local community: Pushed to the periphery, the church leaves a void, also drawing criticism for its perceived irrelevance.

Rendle writes that the encroachment of other fields, and the undermining of ministerial leadership from inside congregations, might have good results in the end. He writes that ministers now have an opportunity to reclaim their ancient jurisdiction: discernment of life's meaning.[16] Andover Newton made an error in judgment when it completely removed leadership learning for ministry from the congregation, just as the Christian faith misstepped when it allied with empire; similarly, Christian ministry made a mistake when it strayed from its core purposes of community building and spiritual sense-making. Society once relied on the church to provide spiritual guidance to all in the community, but society changed, and the church did not change fast enough. The disintegration of mainline Christianity and its hold on social power provides an opportunity to rethink ministerial leadership for a new, emergent day.

Times Are Changing Everywhere, for Everyone

All professional fields—from journalism to medicine to teaching—are changing due to cultural shifts that are accelerating more quickly than educators for these professions can respond to. One of the many rationales for a new approach to lifelong learning for leadership is that skills become outdated quickly in such times, and educators in graduate schools will need to retool so that they can prepare students to learn throughout their entire careers. To do so, educators must move up one or two levels of abstraction to focus on principles rather than practice. The problem? Reassessment and revision of most fields' principles are long overdue for redevelopment at the most fundamental level. Consider the assertion in the previous section that the main functions ministerial leaders have to offer are (1) building community and (2) fostering meaning making. These two crucial tasks are not to be found within the fundamental principles that currently guide theological education for ministry.

The leadership landscape on which leaders serve and guide their communities cannot be understood without acknowledging not only the fast pace of change but also its multiple levels. Three key areas where change is accelerating—culture-wide and worldwide—are diversity, technology, and institutional governance.

Diversity and Identity Politics

Communities that were once homogenous are now heterogenous. From urban hubs to small towns, the number and variety of faith communities has exploded during the postmodern era. This proliferation of options for living out one's faith is partly a result of migration. Additionally, faith communities have emerged from the shadows after the floodlights of culturally dominant institutions faded. Easier transportation provides individuals with more options to seek out faith communities that match what they believe. It is not uncommon for a person to drive by five churches on their way to the one they attend, which was not true when many of those churches were originally founded. Technology has both enabled and complicated access to like-minded communities.

Religious diversity is by no means the only—or even the most notable—way in which communities and cultures have become more diverse in recent years. Consider the following list of ways in which people can differ from one another:

1. Gender
2. Gender identity
3. Race
4. Ethnicity
5. Age
6. Ability
7. Sexual orientation
8. Sexual identity
9. Language
10. Class
11. Attractiveness
12. Education
13. Personality
14. National origin
15. Intellectual ability

Many of these categories have emerged in wider public discourse only in the last three to five years. Communities have become more diverse ethnically, racially, and religiously than ever before, and everyone in these communities has access to a world of information that was previously unavailable. Instead of relying on a single newspaper that everyone reads, anyone can now choose from hundreds of different perspectives online. Amid the new tribalism described earlier, some people lock onto a single stream of information for themselves, mystifying those around them.

Leaders can help diverse communities find common ground. They can provide settings for moral reasoning and nonviolent discourse. They can guide those who are different from one another toward each other, and then give people tools to communicate without resorting to harsh language or even violence. Many look to their leaders to make the complex simple. However, no one can do that for them, though many would deign to try. Life among others cannot be simple amid such diversity of backgrounds and thought, and any leader who promises to simplify it is lying both to their community and to themselves.

Technology, Connectivity, and Access to Information

Even in settings where demographics remain unchanged, the influx of new ideas has compensated for a lack of diversity by exposing everyone to ideas they would not have heard of a generation ago. Whereas leaders once controlled access to information, they now struggle to keep up with what their communities already know. Sources of conventional wisdom have multiplied, and while they have always contradicted one another, those contradictions now battle in plain sight.

The era of new tribalism, preceding but also coinciding with an era of emergence, could not have arisen without social media. Through the web, people with specific, focused interests can find each other in ways never before possible. Much good has come from that progress in connectivity. Those seeking a partner or spouse have access to dignified settings for meeting those with shared values and interests. Hobbyists and lobbyists connect with their fellow enthusiasts. People suffering from rare illnesses can reach out to others and provide each other information, comfort, and empathy.

The downsides of human connectivity over the internet receive a great deal of attention, as well they should. The web is unregulated and can serve as a space where dangerous ideas are magnified, as in an echo chamber. The potential harm that technological connectivity poses to communities is not to be taken lightly. Without shared news sources, dialogue among neighbors may rely on conflicting narratives about current events. Technology has enabled new levels of unhealthy secrecy, with communication taking place in the shadows, without the purifying properties of public scrutiny. In the virtual world, participants have little sense of responsibility for the words and ideas they share. Unlikely to be held liable for spreading untruths or making inflammatory statements that incite to violence, online commentators stoke conflict with impunity. Negative online behaviors come at a cost: Those who live online often find their appetites and time for cultivating real relationships—shaped by mutual care that goes beyond ideology—diminishing to the point of disappearance.

Technological advances, especially those that keep human beings connected, tend to outpace society's commonly understood ethics governing technology's use. They also place pressure on leaders not only to learn multiple technologies but to adopt any and all that their communities access. Web-based interfaces for gathering people together during the COVID-19 pandemic it made possible to continue the mission in every setting—from schools to companies, to churches, and even to hospital chaplaincy departments caring pastorally for the ill. These technologies also led to a revolution of rising expectations that now drains leaders' time, energy, and resources, which might be better spent in other forms of engagement.

It was unreasonable to expect ministerial leaders to migrate all their activities onto online platforms with no training, notice, or support, but many of them—heroically—did just that. In doing so, they fed the expectations monster. As the pandemic eased, an assumption emerged that ministers would resume all previous functions while continuing their technological ones, with no revisitation of what expectations might be reasonable. Technology, meant to be a tool for human use, became a ball leaders were expected to chase. Ministry, of course, is not the only field deeply affected by changes adopted during the pandemic. Furthermore, several changes in practice have made life easier for ministers, such as evening meetings that now take place online, from the comfort of home.

Technology's capacity to connect people with information and with one another has tremendous potential, and ministers cannot simply ignore these advances. Yet the advances move more quickly than theological education can keep up with, leaving ministers' educators to make difficult decisions about what to teach: technological interfaces or attitudes and aptitudes? The profession of ministry is not skill-based; skills serve the mission, so ministers need them, but students must first learn about how to serve a mission before those skills make any sense. Canned skills quickly outlive their own usefulness, whereas fostering an attitude that values lifelong learning and the adoption of practices that maximize efficiency in mission fulfillment lasts a lifetime. That said, the wider community does not see their leader's attitude; they see the skills and practices—and they level demands based on those visible signs of competence. Theological educators are therefore under increased pressure to teach the skills communities say they need—and do need—from their ministers. Imparting a value for lifelong learning and the adoption of technologies is a better investment of educators' time amid an already overflowing theological curriculum.

Institutional Governance

Rising Expectations for Transparency and Omnicompetence

Just as human communities have become more mixed—requiring nuance in leaders' approaches that were never previously expected—and as technology provides communities with instantaneous, real-time information and access to one another without the need for the leader's convening power, institutional governance has become more complicated, too. Hierarchies that were once top-down now look like matrices of intersecting accountabilities. This complexity calls for sharing power, which will likely prove healthy for institutions in the final analysis. Sharing leadership, and doing so while all eyes are upon them, places pressure on leaders who are doing something their predecessors never had to do.

Managing amid communal life requires leaders to manage up, manage down, and work as good colleagues to peers. They must figure out all these dynamics—quickly and on the job—without having been taught during their graduate theological education that these practices are important. Their mentors did not need to share their power, nor did they teach their mentees to do so. Their seminaries did not instruct them on the importance of transparency. In fact, some pedagogies that emphasize the transmission of knowledge from scholar to student give the impression that the person with power holds all the cards. Today's ministers must quickly learn to read power dynamics and lead with nuanced attention to them. They must lead as open books, rather than giving the impression that they hold secret expertise, no matter how much that air of mysteriousness and withholding might elevate their status. Technology, combined with expectations for transparency, means that the ministerial leader must learn their job and their context while under intense scrutiny, increasing the degree of difficulty under which they perform their duties.

Institutions operate on different planes of existence in real time, as leaders must attend to the real-life community, the online community, the cataloguing of the past, and the envisioning of the future simultaneously. Institutions require good governance, financial management, fundraising, communications, and membership management, to say nothing of carrying out and achieving a mission. Amid such institutional complexities, the leader often feels like an airplane pilot monitoring a hundred dials. When turbulence hits, their capacity to read all those dials diminishes, and today, turbulence is more the norm than the exception.

Ministerial leaders do well to engage in regular self-reminders and accountability exercises that put their missions front and center. All their multidirectional management serves a purpose, after all. Sometimes, the functions of ministry take on a life of their own. Rather than serving the mission, those functions themselves become needy and demanding. For example, leaders must be transparent regarding how they use their power, but if the community demands that they both carry out their responsibilities and report every decision they make to that community, the leader will run out of time to serve. Regularly returning to a mission statement and strategic plan can help, as such documents provide guidance to leaders on when to say "yes" and when to say "no." Revisiting the roles of various partners in institutional leadership regularly can also help.

Most institutions have a staff, a board, and constituents with rights and responsibilities. In faith communities, the staff is typically composed of those paid or authorized to carry out ministry responsibilities. A board usually includes elected stakeholders tasked with guarding the mission of an institution. They appoint and hold accountable the executive leader, and they provide counsel and correction when the mission requires it. Their work is essential to the task of keeping the organization focused on its purpose in both ordinary and extraordinary times. They are meant to represent the wider constituency of stakeholders and act on their behalf.

Developing a strong and healthy board is something few leaders know how to do when they begin in their roles. The fact that the board (or council, or deacons) is their "boss," appointing them and evaluating them, complicates the work of the minister in cultivating a strong board. Experienced leaders know that they must have board buy-in for their bigger decisions, particularly for changes they wish to make. But how does a leader gather the experience needed to know that buy-in is important, and under what circumstances? How does a minister navigate situations where the board and the broader constituency do not seek the same priorities? Where do they learn to work in settings of shared governance? Learning how to work with a governing board happens mostly on the job. Therefore, leaders must cultivate good skills for learning on the job quickly and in such a way that the mission does not suffer for the leader's inexperience.

One would think that, in a society shaped by new challenges related to diversity, chronic and constant crises, and fast-paced technological advances, constituents would cut their leaders some slack. Basic expectations for compassion would suggest that those in a leader's care would understand that all leaders are facing the same complexities they are. Ultimately, however, human beings tend to project a parental role onto those who are "in charge," especially when they feel anxious. Anxiety—amid climate collapse, violence, and division—is constant for the culture as a whole. Leading transparently from the middle, while under a microscope, presents challenges in a time when expectations of leaders remain fixed and high. Although implementing such an approach can be unusually challenging, a transparent, flat-hierarchy-driven model of leadership remains the most promising practice for uniting communities today.

Conclusion

Ministerial leadership education has a history, a present, and a future. Historically, leadership learning took place through observation, osmosis, and mimesis. More recently, ministry learners have engaged in supervised on-the-job training or taken a course or two during their graduate theological education. However, the usefulness of these more recent approaches to ministerial leadership has already shifted. In the late twentieth and early twenty-first centuries, internships and minimal leadership coursework equipped students with what they needed to lead effectively. Today, their most important function is to prepare future ministers to become lifelong leadership learners. The greatest contribution theological education can make to ministerial leadership education is to instill in students an appreciation for colleagues, an awareness of available learning resources, and a commitment to continuous and intentional growth.

Diversity, complexity, and societal expectations could overwhelm even the most seasoned and prepared leader. Lifelong learning is no antidote for the anxieties these cultural patterns evoke, but it can empower leaders who might otherwise feel swamped and in over their heads. Cultivating competence begins with understanding and accepting the fact that no leader knows everything. A positive attitude toward learning—rather than defensiveness in the face of what they do not know—serves leaders well, now more than ever.

CHAPTER TWO

The Changing Context for Faith Leaders

INSTITUTIONS OF HIGHER learning and field-specific professional guilds carry cultural responsibility for educating competent leaders for society's institutions. Most professional fields' educational formation processes and programs break down into two categories: basic education and lifelong learning. Both might include content, experiential learning, and identity formation, but the emphases of the two phases differ. Basic education usually centers on content, and lifelong learning addresses more nuanced topics related to new challenges facing leaders in the field. Schools and professional guilds both struggle to ensure that those who serve in their areas of concern are up to the task. Both must change, as the culture has changed around them.

Settings for Ministerial Leadership Learning

Independent seminaries and university-embedded divinity schools (to be described hereafter as "seminaries" as an overarching term for graduate theological education) provide much of the basic, foundational education ministers need. They build on both the discipleship formation available to laypersons in the church and the cognitive formation for analytical approaches to complex questions higher education provides. Seminary educators guide the creation and implementation of the curriculum learners experience.

Denominational judicatory officials carry responsibility for assessing the suitability for ministry of those who have been theologically educated. Then, they provide both lifelong learning and accountability management for those authorized to serve under their denominations' auspices. They set forth the criteria for who may become authorized for ministry—"ordained"—in their traditions, and those criteria that guide professional development. Lifelong learning addresses the need to provide resources so that ministers serving in the field may continue to meet expectations as times change.

Notoriously siloed, one from the other, theological schools and denominational judicatory agencies face similar challenges in carrying out their work, providing the education for the lifelong learning religious leaders need and facilitating access to it. An obvious solution would be for the two responsible parties—schools and denominations—to work together more closely.

That said, the culture as a whole broadly assumes that responsibility for the base layer of professional education belongs to higher education, and quality control for professionals belongs to trade guilds. Law schools educate future lawyers, but they do not administer bar exams. Doctors learn to practice medicine in medical schools but must pass medical board exams to be licensed to care for patients. Law schools and medical schools might resource professional guilds as they provide required continuing education that enables lawyers and doctors to hold on to their standing, but choices regarding what trade guilds include in their lifelong learning curricula align not with the basic curriculum of professional schools, but with licensure requirements.

Fighting broadly held assumptions about which educational function belongs under which purview costs energy that neither seminaries nor denominations have to spare. Both seminaries and denominational judicatory agencies can, however, use similar frameworks for imagining a curriculum that prepares ministerial leaders, both at the start of their service and over the course of their lives. That curriculum may continue to include an intense, basic theological education for ministry, coupled with lifelong learning designed for professionals. That said, an assumption well worth fighting is that those in their first phase of professional education and lifelong learners are fundamentally different in how they learn.

Seminaries provide theological education for ministry, along with some professional development, while denominations continue that growth with a focus on ensuring that the clergy who represent their tradition are up to the task of meeting society's need for competent religious leaders. Both seminaries and denominational judicatory agencies adjust their content and delivery systems regularly, but whether change is happening fast enough, or in the right directions, is an open question. Suffice it to say that worry is appropriate.

Those who lead graduate schools of theological education seek to align what they teach with what the world needs from its religious leaders, and the world's needs are nothing if not a moving target. Denominational judicatory agency officials struggle to support clergy who are overburdened and unprepared for the challenges they face. Both theological educators and judicatory officials are within their rights to feel overwhelmed, both by the number of changes to which those in their care must adjust, and by the pace at which those changes are unfolding.

Tectonic Shifts in Seminary Education

Like other professional schools, where the profession in question has changed, theological education must catch up with society's needs for and in its religious leaders. Education lags behind the requirements of the field. Catching up will not be easy, due to ground shifting in numerous ways and directions.[1] In Christianity's first two millennia, models for theological education varied widely. The early church required no formal education for ministry, and postgraduate seminary education is an innovation of the past two hundred years.[2] At this moment, the field is either mid-shift or at the early stages of a new era, yet the basic theological curriculum and the lifelong learning provided by denominations remain largely unchanged from the modern era.

Seasoned theological educators might wonder, when hearing the sense of urgency coming from those early in their careers, what all the fuss is about. "We thought the church was coming to an end, too, in the 1960s," they say. "It bounced back then, and it will bounce back now." They might be right, but the number and nature of the challenges the Christian church faces today are different from those of the mid- to late twentieth century. Changes are bigger, and they are coming at institutions faster, creating challenges whose sheer magnitude has not been seen before.

Religion's Fading Cultural Relevance

Today's ministerial leaders and those who educate them and assess their fitness navigate change on a landscape where the jury is out as to whether religion even matters, and therefore whether ministry, as a field, has a future. The church has a long history of waxing and waning, with repeated predictions that future generations would not sustain it. This time, the predictions might be right or might be wrong, but anxieties about that future affect everything seminary educators do.

Whereas ecumenical dialogue might have been the new horizon of the 1960s and 1970s, and interreligious cooperation the new endeavor of the early 2000s, today's churches must confront the fact that "None" is the fastest growing religious identity in the United States, and many who grew up in the church now categorize themselves as "Done." With each new generation, the likelihood that an adult grew up in an entirely nonreligious household will grow, and signs of generational distance from religious upbringings are beginning to show in the form of nonparticipation in communal religious ritual.

The COVD-19 pandemic shook churches to their core. Although some fared better than others in post-COVID-19 recovery, the Christian movement was not nimble enough to provide a common prophetic voice amid a terrible existential crisis in America. The secularism of US society today, coupled with negative impressions of religion as it relates to politics and war, might indicate new and uncharted waters. Seminary professors do not have experience in teaching students how to make a case for why religion matters, yet ministerial leaders who cannot make that case are ill equipped to lead in the era of the "Nones" and "Dones."

Such graduates will be even less well equipped when ministering to those raised by "None" and "Done" parents, as is the case with many Americans in their teens and twenties today.

Religious leaders must be better educated than at any time in the recent past if they are to explain and defend the importance of religion and how it connects to the creation of a satisfied, meaningful life. They must know the tradition so well that they can transmit it creatively and meaningfully to those who feel no social pressure to participate in it, and who have no language for describing a spiritual experience. When religion's relevance is not taken as a given, however, the societal need for an educated clergy falls under scrutiny that undermines the formation of clergy ready to defend the relevance of a life of faith.

When the body politic questions the necessity of the existence of a sector and its institutions, it is only natural that the public further questions the need for educated professionals to serve those institutions. Were the members of a community to question the need for schools for children, they would not likely embrace education for teachers, especially if that education were expensive to learners and to higher education institutions that receive donated money and federal support via student loans. The same logic applies to religion but whereas a need for schools for children is a broadly held assumption, the necessity of churches for individuals and families is no longer taken for granted.

Even those who avowedly embrace religion and religious leadership as necessary and good have serious questions about the necessity of graduate theological education. Some faiths' ordaining bodies, including those with a long tradition of high expectations for intellectual-powerhouse preachers, have demonstrated their dissatisfaction with the status quo. Mainline Protestant traditions that once required the master of divinity for ordination now accept candidates who have become prepared for ministry through lived experience and a combination of various forms of nondegree learning.

Thus, questions about the need for theological education do not just come from outside the church, but from within it. Those who live entirely outside the church do not think about education for its leaders at all. Those within the church, especially the Protestant mainline, have questions. They wonder about the influence of the academy on Christian thinking, especially as higher education comes under scrutiny in new ways. Both churched and unchurched North Americans have the same two questions about theological education as they do about higher education in general: Are institutions providing education relevant to what society needs, and why are their operations so incredibly expensive?

Mistrust of Colleges and Universities

North Americans no longer generally and universally trust higher education. They no longer assume colleges and universities are forces for good, providing guidance to society through new knowledge and accumulated wisdom. Consider the example of elite university presidents' responses to the 2023 war in Israel and Gaza. Students in some cases said terrible things about Jewish and Muslim people at the onset of the war between Israel and Hamas. Muslim and Jewish students alike felt unsafe physically and emotionally on their campuses. College presidents summoned to Washington, DC, to testify to Congress about antisemitism, bungled their answers to basic questions about student safety versus free speech.

Under pressure to stay out of trouble, they spoke in "legalese," not the language of "leadership." Criticism of university presidents' wishy-washiness laid bare the separation between the academy and the culture. The public likely wanted to trust the academy to provide meaning and moral clarity, but higher education today does not provide that societal voice, beholden as it is to principles of academic freedom and critical inquiry. American society no longer views religion as relevant, and it cannot trust the academy to make meaning. Where, then might society look for narratives that define communal, shared experience? Community members scour the internet and social media platforms looking for answers, and people do not seem able to find answers in the knowledge created in, and preserved and shared through, either the academy or the church.

Furthermore, North Americans generally wonder whether higher education teaches its students or prepares its graduates for the working world of today. Some of the wealthiest Americans, such as Microsoft founder Bill Gates, dropped out of college because they could not find relevant learning for what they felt called to do. Some technologies move so quickly that a computer science student in college is not likely to keep up with counterparts who are learning independently outside the academy, as their faculty members do not know as much about the newest technological applications as they can find online through peers around the world.

An education in the liberal arts is meant to shape a mind so that, when new challenges arise, the graduate can approach them critically, appreciatively, reflectively, and creatively. Over time, universities have come to emphasize job readiness, with liberal arts served as a side dish to the preprofessional main course. Why should preprofessional education take place primarily in a classroom, rather than through an apprenticeship at the leading edge of the field? A case can be made that reading classic literature and studying history must take place in a classroom setting, with wise professors and engaging classmates provoking new and deeper thinking. Such a case is harder to make when educating for the workforce, where removing learners from the field and distancing them from those who know it best defies logic.[3]

The structure of higher education in North America became what it is today through gradual adjustments over a long period of time. In its earliest days, higher education looked like this: Students completed a basic, compulsory, general "secondary" education to prepare them for basic societal functioning. Some went on for four more years of schooling—"higher education"—to sharpen their minds and equip them with knowledge for societal leadership. A smaller number went on to postgraduate education, preparing to lead society's leaders in different sectors and advance society in new directions. This general arc for higher education remains intact, with the important exception being the soaring numbers of those involved in it. Its structures closely resemble those of two hundred years ago, and they have never undergone a major, systemic rethink. Such revision is long overdue, and the need for revisitation of fundamental assumptions about higher education only intensifies as technology becomes more advanced.

Educators did not have to ask the question "What benefit comes from students sitting together, in the flesh, in a classroom with their instructors?" because that was the only way people could come together. Today, the option *not* to be together in the flesh is not only viable but suddenly essential. Professors who assign students writing assignments never had to wonder what benefit to students' minds resulted from the actual process of writing. Did students become more intelligent as they selected words, constructed sentences, and chose evidence to support their positions? With artificial intelligence, writers need only a prompt to generate all of those component parts of a written essay. What gets lost? What could be gained?

The importance of an incarnate community of learners, and the developmental benefit of writing, are two examples of current concerns on the minds of those who design educational programs. They land on top of numerous unresolved questions that previous generations left to be addressed later, by future generations. Some of those questions have become so urgent that evidently, "later" is "now." Like many campus buildings, higher education curricula suffer from deferred maintenance to the point where tearing down and rebuilding might soon become the only logical option.

Eligibility and expense constitute the two broadest categories of concern in higher education. Who should have access to postsecondary education? Past assumptions regarding answers to that question have included "those who are especially intelligent" and "those who can afford it." Underlying those past assumptions are veiled biases connected to class, national origin, race, and gender. Today, the general societal attitude toward higher education is that everyone should be eligible, but the systems managed by educational leaders were not built for everyone. Furthermore, American society does not require a body politic in which everyone is educated the same way. Therefore, how must educators and other cultural leaders rethink eligibility? No easy answers are on offer.

Questions of expense are closely related to questions of eligibility. Some individuals and families possess means to pay for postsecondary schooling. Some rely on the state and loans. Both individuals and governmental leaders question how higher education has become so expensive; yet, when competing for paying customers—children from families of means—colleges and universities face pressure to improve in costly ways. Those improvements do not always align with educational needs, but rather creature comforts and promises of fun that would attract a student with privilege who has many options for where they will spend their tuition dollars. Where neither individuals nor the state provides adequate resources, institutions of higher learning turn to philanthropy, and expectations placed upon those institutions to grow and improve intensify further.

Although different forms of postsecondary and postgraduate education vary in their attractiveness to prospective students of means, their access to government support, and their philanthropic partners' capacity for giving, expectations rise constantly for all educational institutions. On one end, colleges and graduate schools face criticism for how much education in their institutions costs. On the other end, society places expectations on those institutions to educate the populace at the leading edge of every conceivable field of inquiry. Misalignment of expectations between what society expects and what higher education can deliver—at a discount—presents an unsolvable riddle that generations have kicked down the road.

The 2008 mortgage crisis disillusioned Americans who believed everyone had the right to homeownership, and that crisis did so suddenly. Trust in higher education's ability to provide universal access and to prepare well-rounded, wise leaders to carry the body politic into the future has diminished more gradually. Taken together, widespread ambivalence about the relevance of the Christian religion to public and private life, and doubts about higher education's alignment with society's needs, create a difficult—even hostile—environment for educating clergy.

Insufficient Adjustment to Change on the Part of Those with Authority

The field of ministry as a profession has shrunk while being crowded out of the economy due to its structure and its location among professional sectors. Those who study the history of theological education trace its alignment with other professions over time. Andover Seminary (the school served by the author) was the first graduate school of any kind in the US, founded in 1807. Postcollegiate education for professions like law and medicine came later. Now that all purportedly serious professions require postgraduate education, ministry would be loath to give it up, but the painful truth is that the field cannot afford it, given the models for higher education that exist today. Whereas theological education set the pace for education for the professions in the early stages of the Enlightenment, the cultural pressures later forced it to keep up with the Joneses. Today, it is safe to say the race has been lost.

Over the course of North American and European history, ministerial leadership both has and has not mirrored other professional fields. What differentiates clergy from others has changed over time and continues to fluctuate, yet other professions change too.[4] In the early days of the United States, clergy were usually the most educated leaders in their communities. They functioned as "other" on many levels, including their financial lives. Some ministers in the colonies came from families that passed along inherited wealth. Other ministers received holistic support from congregations, which offered pastors parsonages and put food from their farms on pastors' tables. As ministers came to have professional and scholarly peers in their communities, their otherness began to fade, and expectations that ministry was a professional endeavor, like any other, grew.

At the same time, as was described in chapter 1,[5] other fields peeled away from ministry and then began to encroach upon it. Social work and nonprofit management were not professional fields in the early economic landscape of North America. As those fields came into existence and grew, the terrain ministers could call their turf became smaller and smaller. Then, those new fields proved themselves more nimble than the church could allow ministry to be, and were thus better able to adjust to changing needs and times.

One example of the nimbleness of other fields came in the form of what this author refers to as "spectrification." These fields expanded the range of professionals and adjusted the expected education for them in response to increasing complexity. They added specializations and changed the expectations for generalists, then created paraprofessional roles that required less schooling and resulted in lower levels of responsibility. Whereas other professions created various paths that covered the full array of professionals needed—law, for example, broke down into lawyers, paralegals, and legal assistants—religion lacked the economic motivators that would have led to spectrification in ministry or theological education. Christian ministry stubbornly clung to the three-year professional degree, in part because churches are not, for economic reasons, in a position to employ large staffs with differing levels of responsibility and education. Volunteers have always performed staff-level duties in churches, and one cannot rightly expect volunteers to pursue master's degrees, which undermines any attempts at spectrification in seminary education.

Meanwhile, theological education has clung for decades to the master of divinity as the sole qualifier for religious leadership in mainline Christianity, even as the need for more varied levels of preparation has become evident. Instead of demanding variety, the denominations that authorize ministers chose to loosen requirements for seminary education rather than push for new options from their seminaries. Some denominations created schools of ministry, often staffed by educated pastors and retired professors, to take graduate theological education out of the loop entirely. New nondegree ministry schools fulfilled student demand for less time-intensive and more localized educational programs, so seminaries had no incentive to create them.

Consider the counterexample of the medical profession. That field spawned countless specializations, at various levels of education and compensation. Medical boards of examiners did not confront the need for variety by relieving doctors of the necessity of earning a doctor of medicine degree. The field adjusted by creating educational programs that address the spectrum of roles: from the MD/PhD for medical school researchers to the MD and medical specialties for doctors, and to nursing school for nurses, who themselves serve at different levels of required expertise. Surely, the evolution of medical education included challenges and conflicts, but the field adapted. In education for ministry, alignment between education and authorization has not yet taken place in any coordinated way among faith traditions. Given the fragility of seminaries in today's cultural context, such adjustment may be too late.

Professions and the education required for them change in changing times, or they lose their capacity to remain relevant to society, let alone capable of leading that society. Cultural forces have sent unmistakable messages to the church and to theological educators that change in the profession necessitates change in the education that prepares individuals for that profession. Seminaries and denominations have changed, but not necessarily in right and good ways.

Schools that offer graduate theological education have expanded their teaching methods to meet the needs of a widening variety of learners. Like many of postmodernity's institutions, seminaries and divinity schools have adjusted to a body of candidates that are different from one another and different from their historic predecessors. Theological schools adjust to the needs of students in one way: by expanding access to their programs. Simultaneously, denominations adjust in a different way: by discontinuing authorization requirements for theological education at the graduate level. As theological schools *adjust* and denominations *opt out*, the relationships between the entities that educate (graduate theological schools) and those that authorize (denominational ordaining bodies) break down.

Resource scarcity prevents a rapid pivot in graduate theological education. Professional education, no matter the field, is inconvenient and expensive. The United States is waking up to this reality slowly, in fits and starts, as conflict rages over who is responsible for outsized educational debt. Such debates tend to focus on the borrower, but other worthy questions simmer under the surface: Does higher education—collegiate and postcollegiate—benefit the individual receiving the education, or the tax-paying public as a whole? Who, therefore, should pay for that higher education?

Graduate theological schools feel the burden of rising costs more acutely than other institutions of higher learning. They tend to be small, each serving a few faith traditions. Although some schools have experimented with different approaches to finding economies of scale, small seminaries struggle to provide the numerous services accredited schools all require. Seminaries do not have a steady source of dependable income from their constituents, whose abilities to pay vary and who will never earn sufficient wages in ministry to carry heavy debt. In days of yore, churches paid for their young men to attend seminary. Later, Christian denominations supported their seminaries with direct funding. Then, the financial burden fell to students as denominations' funds dwindled. Costs were low enough at first that students could manage them, but as costs rose, those experiencing a call from God, to which many felt they could not say no, took on debt they would not be able to afford to repay.

Existential economic problems face seminaries while the wider culture presents even more overwhelming challenges. Calls for diversity place all historically privileged institutions on notice. They raise appropriate questions regarding Christian privilege across institutions that must be addressed. Because of diversity's intersecting and overlapping nature, new and multilayered questions about diversity challenge theological educators as they simultaneously answer challenges to their work's relevance from Christian insiders. New and important questions include, "Should graduate schools for ministry serve one denominational tradition, or all?"; "What about interreligious education for Muslims, Jewish persons, and those beyond the Abrahamic traditions?"; and "What about the imperialism and racism intertwined with religious history and written into Christian theology?"

Currently, approximately 250 Christian seminaries and divinity schools educate religious scholars and leaders beyond the college years. The three ecclesial families into which they are commonly sorted are mainline Protestant, Evangelical, and Catholic and Orthodox.

Obviously, the US is home to more than 250 Christian denominations, but seminaries have found themselves able to work across traditions, within reason. To have separate theological schools for all Christian expressions would be impractical, so many schools have a long history of building theological flexibility into their programs.

But how much theological flexibility is too much for one institution to bear? On the one hand, the culture calls for more diversity on every level, but on the other hand, Christian leaders without strong identity formation cannot make the case for religion's relevance in a skeptical season. Can Christian conservatives and liberals learn alongside each other when their traditions' very understandings of what it means to be a Christian, let alone a Christian minister, are so dissimilar? To educate all Christians together, without tradition-specific training, presents challenges related to ministerial identity formation, imperiling candidates' ability to serve a particular tradition. As vitriol comes to dominate public discourse, theological educators who seek to teach future ministers from widely varied points of view might find their instructional time siphoned off entirely into conflict management.

Concerns about intra-Christian theological education are only the start. Other valid question are: Why should the wider culture support—through, for example, federal student loan eligibility—a theological education system that educates Christians only? Why should Christianity dominate the landscape of postgraduate higher education in a world increasingly defined by multiple religious views and interreligious conflict? Christian divinity schools and seminaries hold nearly all the resources available for postgraduate theological education in America. No major university has an affiliated Jewish divinity school. Even Harvard Divinity School, with its strong commitment to interreligious education, is historically Christian, as is Harvard's university chapel.[6] Graduate schools of Islam are small in number, mostly new, and mostly unaccredited. Zaytuna College in Berkeley, California, for example, is regionally authorized to grant degrees and to make federal financial aid available to students, but its master of arts degree is not accredited on a national level by the Association of Theological Schools.

On the one hand, few, if any, seminaries or divinity schools have the capacity to educate well those who will serve in a wide range of traditions. On the other hand, dividing students into camps to educate them fails to provide society leaders who can connect across differences in a fragmented world. Fully siloed education for religious leaders, where learners are surrounded with those who share their beliefs, cannot prepare ministry students for a multireligious world. Ministerial leaders from varied traditions must work together in local communities for the sake of world peace, so why not teach them together and inculcate in them a value for cross-tradition collegiality? Both tradition-specific formation and breadth of theological learning are important but fitting both under one tent presents a challenge in curriculum development and community life.

These many challenges named above place pressure on theological schools just as the relevance of religion, as well as the cost–benefit ratio of higher education, are under intense scrutiny culture-wide. Ministerial leadership is difficult work. The more high-quality and appropriate education a person receives, the better they do, yet even such an education cannot guarantee success in a quickly changing field, where the skills and ideas garnered in graduate theological education have short shelf lives. Theological education that takes place over the concentrated years of graduate school cannot be the beginning and end of preparation when the ministry of tomorrow is unknown today.

As graduate theological schools continue to seek to adjust to the times, those who think about education for ministerial leadership effectiveness must consider the needs of the field beyond two- to three-year postgraduate theological education experiences. They must do so not just because not all will receive graduate theological education, but because theological education's necessarily academic content orientation ensures that only lifelong learning can ensure the ability to keep up with changing times.

Ministerial leaders need practices that catalyze learning over the course of a lifetime, for the world around them is changing faster with each passing year. Education for ministry is not simply a matter of professional effectiveness. Ministers' overall happiness and work satisfaction benefit from education that keeps the minister's minds, and their faiths, fresh. No one is more certain to burn out than a minister who feels out of their depth, unready for God to use them to the good.

Problems come at theological educational leaders from all directions. The culture questions the relevance of religion. The economic model for educating clergy is broken. Denominations that authorize ministers are fragile and often dysfunctional. Christianity's dominance is under scrutiny as the US becomes more religiously diverse, and today's leaders are answering for Christianity's historic and present complicity with imperialism and multiple forms of injustice (racism, sexism, and heterosexism to name just three). Yet amid these intersecting crises, God continues to call people to serve in ministry, and the wider community seeks transcendence, meaning, and purpose. Those called to educate clergy cannot throw up their hands in defeat.

Changing Expectations for Leaders

In their book, *The Power Code: More Joy, Less Ego, More Impact for Women (and Everyone)*,[7] Katty Kay and Claire Shipman investigate cultural sources of power. They describe how power is only in small part inherent to a person who holds it and is, in larger part, a construct built of norms and assumptions. *The Power Code* looks closely at a particular dimension of leadership—power—and redefines it as a tool rather than a status. Redefining power forces an examination of assumptions surrounding it. Once one assumption comes under scrutiny, the same light exposes others. Once a person questions what power is, they simultaneously challenge preconceived notions about who should have access to it.

In a similar way, looking closely at a different dimension of leadership—its development—requires self-examination regarding assumptions. Tacit beliefs about what leaders are, and how they become leaders, may no longer stand unchallenged. Shining a light on assumptions about what leaders *are*, and how they *got* where they are, creates possibilities for greater access to the previously ineligible, as tacit assumptions are bound to be discovered to be needlessly narrow.

The "Great Man" Theory of History and Leadership

Biographer Doris Kearns Goodwin writes about great leaders: Abraham Lincoln, Teddy Roosevelt, Franklin Delano Roosevelt, and the Kennedys. In her book, *Leadership in Turbulent Times*,[8] Goodwin considers the journeys of various American leaders through the most difficult years of their careers, examining their choices and actions. The book provides its readers with inspiration but also runs the risk of feeding certain fantasies about leaders' capacities to save society from itself. It lifts up a small number of leaders for their insightfulness and contrasts it with the lack of foresight exhibited by their peers and predecessors. Goodwin presents these figures' stories, with special emphasis on their occasionally counterintuitive choices, in such a way that readers cannot help but hope the genius of those heroes might rub off on them. Goodwin's choice of subjects and focus reflects a "great man" theory of history.

Sam Jacobs, *TIME*'s editor-in-chief, describes the rationale for the magazine's annual "Person of the Year" feature as a belief that individuals can change the course of history.[9] Even this rationale suggests that, while history moves *on occasion* due to an individual, most cultural change happens through collective movements. *TIME*'s Person of the Year tradition dates back to 1927, the height of the modern era and its accompanying humanistic veneration of human potential. After a great man theory of history, a great man theory of leadership—and leadership development—is a next logical mental step. If great men have the power to transform society, those who aspire to transform it should seek to be great men, and one way to do so is to study the actions of great men in history. Despite *TIME*'s own built-in disclaimers, many embrace the idea that society needs heroes more than shared responsibility.

A person who embraces the great man theory of leadership might believe the best way to learn to lead is to examine and replicate the decisions of those who were deemed exceptional. They will choose to read biographies and autobiographies and attend talks by those who have made a difference, borrowing and advancing suggestions drawn from the lives of others. Great leaders have existed in the past, and we search the landscape for them today. Telling their stories helps society to build a shared identity and group cohesion. Reading biographies is a valid means of improving one's leadership practice. Such study provides tips and suggestions, as well as glimmers of hope when times are tough.

That said, studying great leaders reinforces an individualistic, acontextual model for understanding leadership that ultimately does more harm than good to the cause of leadership development. Goodwin's stories provide data but do not reshape the readers' thinking about themselves, the world, and their capacities to effect change. As leadership development practices go, they are insufficient, but for many, they are the only lifelong learning for leadership they receive. Keynote addresses from so-called "successful" people, "inspirational" quotes and aphorisms attributed to important historic figures, and the study of the however-many habits of highly successful leaders—these leadership development practices propose education through mimesis. They might offer some beneficial tips, but they also suggest a definition of leadership that is outdated and largely unattainable. If a leader becomes successful through imitating another leader from the past, their success today could best be described as a lucky break or coincidence.

For today's leaders, effecting change begins as an inside job. A reader might take inspiration from a story of brave actions but cannot expect magical pixie dust to rub off on them from the hero. Why? Because there is no pixie dust. To assume otherwise is to misunderstand the movement of God in human history. Past and present great leaders' stories provide today's leaders with insights into God's work through human agents and offer inspiration to act boldly when God calls them into service. Yet "great men" are no closer to God than anyone else. Only Jesus occupies the space between God's realm and the created world in any permanent way. God breaks into incarnate reality, and when that happens, it is grace: an unearned gift that does not conform to transactional principles of a market economy.

Any seemingly supernatural gifts exhibited by a leader in the past were seen as coming from God and were deployed to God's purpose. "God made use of them, and now God can make use of me," is perhaps the single most useful leadership lesson a person can take from reading the biography of a so-called "great man." Signs point to God deploying today's disciples differently than in the past, serving as they do amid an interconnected, diverse, and global human community. The emerging era calls not for singular heroes but those able to empower others from the grassroots, which begins with relationship.

It is for these reasons that one must take care when investigating the work of effective leaders of the past: They may have useful tactics to share and inspiring stories that energize us, but they are not to be understood as God's messengers in some anointed way. Their very earthliness gives reason to hope that today's leaders can be just as effective if they are wise and prepared to make good choices. The bad news is that focusing too much energy on God's past messenger-servants can bring out the worst in communities as they relate to their leaders. Great men set up expectations for heroics and take responsibility away from the gathered community.

The Christian church, and its related entities, has a checkered past as relates to its veneration of great men. Consider these three examples, coming from the first three churches where this author held membership: the First Church of Christ, Congregational in Suffield, Connecticut; Battell Chapel at Yale University; and the Memorial Church in Harvard Yard.

My parents joined First Church in Suffield when I was a toddler, and I do not remember a time when it was not at the center of our weeks and an important space for our family. The minister of my childhood was J. Gorman Smith. My father and mother adored him, especially because they loved his preaching. I now know that he had his fair share of conflict with members of the congregation. My aunt carried anger with her to her grave over Mr. Smith's decision to remove a wooden cross from the chancel in favor of a backlit stained-glass window. Was my aunt upset due to her (widely shared) anti-Catholic sentiment, given the connection many made between imagery and Papist tendencies? Perhaps, in part, but what seemed to gall her the most was his autocratic choice that led to the removal of an image sacred to her.

We never called our pastor "Rev. Smith" or "Pastor Smith," as we were New England Congregationalists who did not put our ministers on pedestals. That said, we *did* put him on a pedestal, and after Mr. Smith left, my parents—my father, in particular—never fully recovered. They respected other pastors, of course, but there was always something about them that fell short of J. Gorman Smith, whether it was their preaching (which led people to a deeper faith) or their take-no-prisoners style (which led some, like my aunt, to loathe him, and others to admire him for his strength).

The first church I attended after leaving home was Battell Chapel, the University Church at Yale. My chaplains were the Rev. Dr. Harry B. Adams and the Rev. Dr. F. Jerry Streets, and both were important to me in their own ways. I remain close with Dr. Streets, and Dr. Adams and I attended the same church in recent years, leading up to his death. The recently retired Chaplain Sharon Kugler was among my closest colleagues and personal friends in recent years. All these details should tell you that I never knew, or was ministered to by, William Sloane Coffin, but I might as well have been, so present is his spirit at Yale.

William Sloane Coffin made a name for himself as a preacher during the Vietnam War. He preached peace and drew global attention to Yale for his provocative and controversial messages. He was both an icon and an iconoclast, respected and listened to by activists and establishment-lovers alike. I also know that he led the church with little consultation with stakeholders in the congregation or university. He brought the congregation into the United Church of Christ back when the denomination's merger took place—without anyone knowing he was doing so. He did not build up lay leaders and balked at authority, while at the same time gathering power and authority unto himself. He operated with free rein from the pulpit and, likely, everywhere else. He was a giant, and he changed many lives. However, he was also the worst imaginable predecessor for his successors: a Congregationalist cult of personality should be read as an oxymoron if ever there was one, given the low-church interpretation of ordination that characterizes the Congregational way.

When I began divinity school, the first thing I did was start a part-time job as an intern at the Memorial Church in Harvard Yard. The Rev. Peter John Gomes was the preacher to the University. I had never heard of him before I started working for him, and, although my supervisor was his associate, it was clear to me from day one: We all worked for him. I went on to serve the church's staff and, later, was part of the first "chapter" of ministers in the vicinity to become affiliated with the Memorial Church, whose name was and still is synonymous with Rev. Gomes.

Rev. Gomes was not always as famous as he became in the last twenty years of his career and life. He became much better known in the wider public in my second year of service to the church, when *The Good Book: Reading the Bible with Mind and Heart*[10] came out. Previously, Rev. Gomes was known at Harvard for being "more Harvard than Harvard." Outside the university, some had heard of him due to his decision to come out as gay at a rally supporting LGBTQ students in the early 1990s.

Like both the other strong, male leaders named above, Rev. Gomes was a compelling preacher. He had an inimitable style, which ironically inspired many to try to imitate his accent, which he described alternately as "Plimothian" (he hailed from Plymouth, MA) and "Afro-Saxon." He was a shrewd strategist beyond the pulpit and in the university. For example, early in his more than forty-year career at Harvard, he asked if the preacher to the University was expected at faculty meetings, given his membership in that body. He was told no, given that he was untenured, but he showed up for meetings anyway. After many years, no one in those meetings remembered a time when he was not there, and his portrait now hangs in the room where faculty meetings take place at Harvard College.

When Rev. Gomes preached on Sundays, the congregation was packed. When he did not, attendance dropped. When he became ill and died, his associate at the time suggested he be lain in state for mourners. Although many—including myself—thought the idea macabre, hundreds of visitors lined up to pay their last respects. Serving on the search committee for Rev. Gomes's successor, I heard many times, "No one would want to succeed Peter Gomes." Oh, how mistaken they were! He had carved out a cultural position others envied and desired, but many still believe there will never be another like him.

What made the acts of these three charismatic, inspiring figures hard to follow? What made them special? Of course, these men were talented and educated individuals of wisdom and character. But they were also products of their time, and they became products of the imaginations of those to whom they ministered. They were great men who made their congregations feel safe, much like a person feels safe in the presence of a parental figure who frames and explains reality to a community. In times of uncertainty, their giant personalities represented a cosmic grown-up who would make everything okay.

Some institutions have a great leader at their helm, and that leader motivates the community to step up, share leadership, and serve without counting the cost. Other institutions have great leaders who cause the rest of the community to recede in ways that are unhealthy for everyone, including the spiritual leader, the community, and the leader's successor. The spiritual leader who rests on their laurels is not likely to adapt to the needs of the times, becoming less and less helpful to the organization as their skills and behaviors become less relevant. The community suffers when the great man (who need not be male-bodied) fosters dependency.

The successor to the great man might pay a higher price than anyone, as they are forced to make long-overdue changes to the institution that might be unpopular during the early period of their ministry, when they are trying to build trust in their leadership. They must take actions that are bound to feel swift to the community, but those moves are necessary because they are driving the institution out of a rut. The community might fear that these changes will be destructive, as it is not used to any changes at all. Furthermore, the great man's successor inherits a group of codependents seeking another companion in that codependency. Only the most mature and savvy leader can break the cycle. Many simply adopt the codependency their predecessor enjoyed, perpetuating the great-man cycle, until the community realizes that their new leader is not the same great man. They then become disappointed in the new leader for not being like the one before, and the organization stagnates instead of embracing a new person and a new time.

The harm often left behind by great men goes beyond emotional codependence. Great men tend to neglect empowering spiritual growth and do not take the time and energy to develop the leaders around them. Two things thus go wrong: Agency deteriorates, and institutions become ingrown. Some charismatic leaders tacitly empower those in their care to hand over agency for their own spiritual lives to the leader. In extreme cases, that relinquishing agency over the relationship between the individual and God turns the charismatic leader into a cult leader. In more ordinary cases, the compelling spiritual leader occupies so much space in the minds of those in their care that the leader and the followers' faiths blend into one another. Agency is important for adult faith development. The less invested a person is in growing in their own relationship with God, and the more ready they are to glom onto the charismatic leader, the thinner their commitment to their faith will become. One pastoral turnover can be enough to snip that thin thread, taking away not just a person's pastor, but their church, or even their faith in God.

Healthy ministerial leaders encourage a sense of ownership in the faith community among all they serve, including members and other designated leaders. Whether for reasons of ego or because they have come to believe their own press, great men rarely dedicate adequate time to building up the leaders around them. The best thing a charismatic leader can do to ensure the success of their successor is to surround the one who follows with wise, spiritually mature leaders who feel responsible for the institution. Leadership transition in any organization requires a strong network of healthy leaders below the executive level, giving the new chief time to become established and able to model for the new leaders what commitment to the mission looks like.

When the charismatic leader departs and no one is prepared to step up to facilitate and support the transition, the institution can become ingrown. A tree's root system needs to push down as its branches spread upward so that the tree achieves and sustains balance. In the same way, a faith community with a charismatic leader must attend to deepening all leadership roles, rooting downward through spiritual and leadership development for all, not just the one whose branches are on vivid display. Without such deepening, neither a tree nor an institution can weather storms; and transition is always stormy. The great man who does not develop their board, staff, and volunteers will topple in strong winds or perish when the seasons change.

The great man theory of leadership remains alive and well in the minds of many, if not most, institutions today. Left unexamined, tacit assumptions steer the community's thinking about what a leader is and should do. Many communities suffer from chronic anxiety amidst the intersecting crises that shape communal life. Those who are anxious seek a rescuer, and their leaders must tend to that anxiety without allowing the community to sustain the delusion that anyone can save an institution from the need for deep change. Healthy leaders must disabuse communities of the notion that they have the magic solution that will take anxiety away, and at the same time they must empower communities so they might come to realize they do not need saving from anyone, as God has already saved all creation.

Leaders cannot pull their communities away from an obsessive belief in great men who can save them simply by telling them to let go of it. By the time a group of people is suffering from existential anxiety that their organization is in danger and needs a human savior, it is too late for explanations. Instead, leaders must engage in the long-term work of deepening the organization's roots: tending to spiritual and leadership development; changing the community with the times, rather than skimming over hard choices; and spreading out rather than hoarding opportunities to take part in visible, engaging, and meaningful work.

Leaders who function well in a season of emergence share authority and responsibility with other stakeholders. They embody authenticity, honesty, and transparency, and they draw the same behaviors out of others. They collaborate and partner at every opportunity. They dedicate time to building relationships within their community, especially with its other leaders. They tell the community stories about itself, so its members know what the community is and what it can become. The story is not about the leader, but about all the community has survived and achieved.

Leaders who serve communities that want them to become the "great man" who is also the man of their dreams must reshape those projections into mirrors, whereby those who shine unearned trust onto their charismatic leaders see a glow in themselves. A savvy leader can play with the great-man hopes and dreams of the community to help them to see possibilities. Such play might include using the latitude usually extended to the great man to introduce a new idea that might not otherwise gain traction. Playing with great man paradigms in an attempt to move the institution forward could involve reintroducing rituals of pomp and circumstance that seem to center the leader but which ultimately cause the whole community to shine with pride.

When used to serve the mission, a top-down and hierarchical style of leadership can ethically rest among the many tools in the leader's toolbox for effecting change. But the danger of overusing such tools is not to be underestimated. Leaders must always remember that they do not have all the answers, no matter how much their constituents wish and believe they do. When leaders feel insecure, this self-awareness can be difficult. The leader tempted to take advantage of the transferred, the unexamined trust the community places in them will ultimately lead to disappointment when new ideas go wrong. Taking the credit today means taking the blame tomorrow.

Today's communities need a different set of gifts and practices from their leaders than was the case in a less complicated, more hierarchical historic moment. Not all communities are aware of that fact or ready to accept it. They look for a great man who can swoop in and fix all that is wrong with communities, institutions, and the world. Keeping that dream alive may make the leader feel special and confident in the short term, but that fantasy ultimately undermines the healthy leader's effectiveness. The life-giving practices related to sharing leadership and fostering spiritual vitality might decenter the ministerial great man, but they are essential to organizational health.

Ladder Theories of Progress

The story of the Christian movement offers examples of communities making faulty assumptions about what progress looks like. Consider the account in Genesis 11:1–9 of God's people making bad choices in an attempt to excel by creating a physical structure that put them on God's level:

> Now the whole earth had one language and the same words. And as they migrated from the east, they came upon a plain in the land of Shinar and settled there. And they said to one another, "Come, let us make bricks, and burn them thoroughly." And they had brick for stone, and bitumen for mortar. Then they said, "Come, let us build ourselves a city, and a tower with its top in the heavens, and let us make a name for ourselves; otherwise we shall be scattered abroad upon the face of the whole earth." The Lord came down to see the city and the tower, which mortals had built. And the Lord said, "Look, they are one people, and they have all one language; and this is only the beginning of what they will do; nothing that they propose to do will now be impossible for them. Come, let us go

> down, and confuse their language there, so that they will not understand one another's speech." So the Lord scattered them abroad from there over the face of all the earth, and they left off building the city. Therefore it was called Babel, because there the Lord confused the language of all the earth; and from there the Lord scattered them abroad over the face of all the earth.

Scholars who write about history and leadership in Western culture have long debunked what is known as the "ladder theory of progress." Ladder theories are all about excelling and reaching, even when doing so involves climbing over others on the way up. Ladder theories are tempting to those who want a clear definition of goals and success. They also tend to give way to rampant capitalistic competition, which in turn leads to disparities of wealth and, eventually, oppression. Least obviously, but most nefariously, ladder theories of progress fail to take the rapidity of cultural change into consideration. Those who define goals in terms of linear and single-variable definitions of progress are the most vulnerable, like the confused inhabitants of the Tower of Babel, to becoming scattered from one another.

Ladders are not stable structures. While they have an important job, they are defined by their instability as much as their utility: If one builds one's definition of success on a ladder, one will be vulnerable to catastrophic falls, especially if that ladder was built quickly and shoddily. The ladder theory of progress employs what turns out to be an apt metaphor: Ladders might move in an upward direction, but they are fragile in their linearity. They fall due to the whims of weather, gravity, human clumsiness and imbalance, and uneven ground. Collapse is the inevitable result of a model for human progress that relies on a ladder theory of progress.

In the summer of 2023, a building collapsed in New Haven, Connecticut.[11] Some workers poured cement into one of the new building's floors more quickly than the other workers could spread it around. The cement broke through the web of andirons that held the floor together, and everything fell through. Workers were injured and hospitalized. Construction came to a halt not just in this building but throughout the region, as investigators examined whether faulty materials caused the accident. The metaphor speaks loudly: When leaders go too fast, take on too much, and are not on the same page with their partners in mission, collapse is bound to happen.

Governments, banks, buildings, and markets collapse regularly and seem to be doing so at an alarming rate in a culture of fast-moving change. The church as Western culture knows it today is collapsing or has already collapsed, at least partially. The church is collapsing insofar as it has embraced practices similar to those of governments, banks, and markets in order to survive and influence the cultures of its various eras. In its understandable attempts to keep up with other sectors of the economy and civic life, it made the same mistakes other institutions made by embracing imperial and economic power. The church needed to adapt to survive, and some of its mimicry of democracy and markets was good. However, some was bad, such as selecting forms of decision-making that favor the will of the powerful over the needs of the vulnerable, or by trusting markets to regulate all social needs.

Ladders are fragile because they lack breadth and foundational stability. Good leadership today, therefore, calls for heightened attention—now more than ever, in an age when systems are collapsing right and left—to evenness, balance, and groundedness. Groundedness, in the case of the church, refers to the good news of love and life that God created and that human beings, therefore, cannot destroy. Christian leadership is grounded on the solid foundation of the gospel: an ethic of resurrecting love. The gospel is not fragile. God's love, and only God's love, is too big to fail.

New metaphors and images for leadership growth must demonstrate building not just upward, but outward, inward, and in every direction that leads to balance and rootedness. Shapes provide important metaphors for describing the nature of leadership. A ladder signifies movement in an upward direction with little regard for foundational breadth. It also suggests linearity, as the two supports that contain the rungs run parallel to one another, never expanding or converging. As an image for leadership development, it gives the impression that one

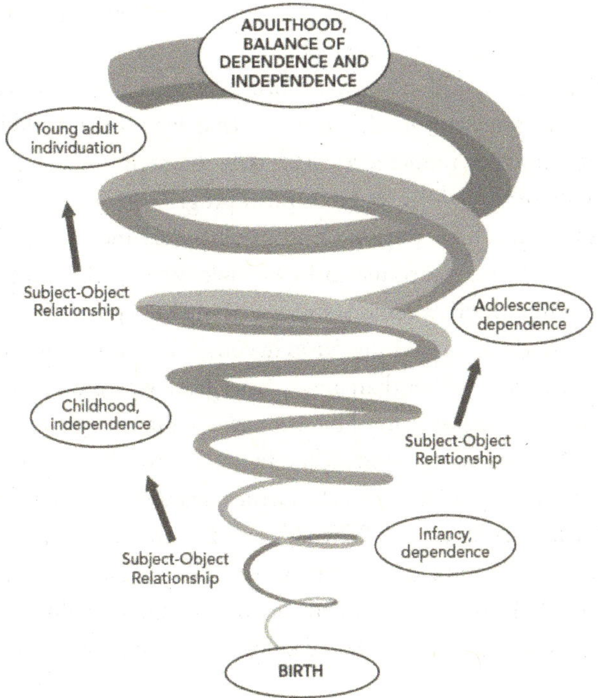

Figure 2.1.[12]

can move up in the world while moving in only one direction without fundamentally changing.

Other shapes provide more helpful images for well-rounded, continuous leadership development. One shape used to describe human development comes from Robert Kegan, a scholar of adult development at the Harvard Graduate School of Education. The shape is a three-dimensional conical space, held in by an expanding coil:

Even without going into detail about the theory presented in Figure 2.1, the sturdiness of its shape suggests an apt alternative image to a ladder. The developmental model Kegan proposed suggests growth in multiple directions, both upward and outward. The spiral indicates movement through time, but the fact that the spiral is conical rather than cylindrical shows that growth may be cyclical, yet developing humans never return to the same developmental point twice. For example, a Christian might cycle through the liturgical year, but each time they return to the same season, they discover that even if the world has not changed (though it almost surely has), they themselves have changed.

The shape of a ladder suggests linear progress in one direction and captures a capitalistic notion of progress, where more capital is the goal. Other theoretical frameworks for civic life take different shapes, and thus offer different options for describing life's purpose and goals. Marx's dialectical materialism moves in consciousness-raising loops and results in outward, rather than upward, progress, where all thrive. Similarly, mid-twentieth-century liberation theologians in Latin America promoted class consciousness, wherein awareness of the arbitrariness and unhealthiness of top-down class structures could cure an otherwise insatiable hunger for capital. When liberated, both the rich and the poor would come to recognize the interconnectedness of everyone's fate. The shape of a dialectically developed worldview is not a ladder, nor is it reliant on a great man. It is egalitarian and built to grow horizontally.

The Fundamental Insufficiency of Goal Orientation in Leadership and Its Development

The shape of things to come for ministerial leadership development will not be a ladder. "Do more, and do it better," is a meaningless goal. "More" and "better" require a referent to the past, and harking back to the past does not honor the urgent calls of the present and future. "More" is already drowning humanity in data that overwhelms leaders. "Better" suggests that the current direction is the right one, and that a good leader merely pushes toward it more quickly. Ministerial leaders suffer when they and their constituents imagine human goals to be more important than discerning the work of the Holy Spirit. Yet such imaginings are common. Ministers in institutional settings often answer to boards that include powerful leaders from other, more powerful—namely, more competitive—sectors of the economy.

As ministry as a profession mistakenly adopted the trappings of other professions in the culture as a means of protecting its cultural relevance in the modern era, it took on the language of goal orientation. Now, that language is letting leaders down across fields. In a fast-moving, data-overloaded, conflict-heavy world, goal orientation can lead to despair. When professionals set goals today, they do so with insufficient information, unknown obstacles, and the likelihood that any change they seek will take place in a landscape that is changing even faster, in ways they do not know or understand. A new model for leadership development must include concepts of balance and the possibility that the leader *is*, and is *doing*, enough.

Likewise, great men will not shape the future. In fact, it is unclear whether they ever truly shaped the past or if history simply told civic stories that centered on individuals out of modernist enthusiasm for heroes. Today's great men are not so much inspiring as they are terrifying. The damage they are capable of knows no bounds. Blind trust in technocrats and blind loyalty to autocrats strip the wider culture of its capacity to think critically and act creatively. When conflicts take place between authoritarians, lives are lost. Threats of violence against those who defy today's great men frighten and thus silence the public.

Despite the insufficiencies of the great man theory of history and leadership, and the potential for disappointment built into ladder theories of progress, both introductory and continuing education for professions still reflect these outdated notions of human development. Higher education remains individualistic, information-driven, and isolated from the fields professionals will go on to serve. "More" and "better" are rewarded. "Balance" and "enough" are foreign concepts. Higher education's emphasis on setting and attaining goals carries over into all of society's leadership functions. Goals take the form of acquiring and achieving, rather than finding wholeness and lifting up all in the community.

This disconnect between what society needs and the way society's leaders are formed, presents a danger to ministry as a profession and to the education that prepares them. Ironically, it is because of the other ways in which theological education is already broken that theological educators now have an opportunity to repair that disconnect, as they have no choice but to rebuild. Built on a broken economic model and outdated assumptions about religion in society, theological education, as it is currently known, is collapsing. This collapse makes space and offers cultural permission to do something new, perhaps even out of the raw materials scattered on the ground.

Conclusion

Education for ministry must untether itself from the unrealistic and unhealthy assumptions—individualism, competition, and the pursuit of capital—that shape, and are undoing, other fields. Then, the ministerial leader must tend to the souls of those who continue to cling to unhelpful and outdated models that suggest professionals are defined by what they do, how much they earn, and whom they defeat. The world calls for ministerial leaders who are grounded, balanced, present, and receptive to the work of the Holy Spirit in real time. Their formation for leadership must take a new and different shape from what has come before. That shape must reflect a Christian understanding of human wholeness, where all are beloved, yet only God is God.

Part II

Intentionality

Approaches to Developing Faith Leaders

CHAPTER THREE

A Theoretical Framework for Ministerial Leadership Development

In a season of overwhelm, when no leader believes themselves to be enough or to be doing enough, a new theoretical framework for leadership development is needed. Such a framework provides guardrails and guidelines so that leaders can engage in ongoing growth in a manner they can sustain while carrying out their responsibilities. Leaders are working in a time when ongoing education has never been more important, due to the rapidly changing culture that surrounds them and the institutions in their care. At the same time, religious leaders in particular have never been less trusted. They must therefore demonstrate their competence while under scrutiny and without the benefit of the doubt.

In the not-too-distant past, ministers learned to lead on the job. Their formal education included book learning: sacred text, ancient languages, theological doctrines. They graduated into settings where they had mentors built in, as most ministers served as part of a team—at least at first. Those who did not have good mentoring could rely on shared cultural understandings of their role in the communities they served. Congregation members could pass on that cultural understanding to newer ministers, and they did so supportively, wanting to be led and wanting their ministers to succeed.

Effective leaders found accidental success through a combination of innate gifts, substantial education on the Christian tradition, a world that hungered to hear their message (or at least pretended to, in the interest of cultural acceptance), and willing followers. Many of these past ministerial leaders stumbled into balanced, curated leadership development programs that served them well in the absence of a guiding theoretical framework: As the most educated persons in town, they were expected to read and research. Even those who intuitively came to a realization that they needed to stay current on information, deepen their reflection, and expand their horizons in order to maintain their effectiveness would no doubt have benefited from a more structured approach.

In the modern era in Western societies, spanning from the mid-nineteenth to mid-twentieth centuries, societal leadership was specific and defined. A leader brought people together and pointed them in a direction deemed "good" by the standard of the shared values of those who controlled resources. That leader guided the community in the indicated direction, overcame obstacles along the way, and guarded the values of the elite from those who might question them. Call top-down, authoritative leadership what you will—efficient? oppressive?—but no one questions its clarity or the efficiency that results from that clarity. A ministry's success or failure depended on whether the leader could guide a community down a predetermined path. In *Leadership for a Changing Church: Charting the Shape of the River*,[1] ministerial leadership scholar Robert Dale writes that all leaders needed to adjust to new expectations at the dawn of the postmodern era in the 1960s. Industrial-age leaders made products, whereas information-age leaders were called upon to make sense. Dale argued that clergy have an edge in a sense-making desert, where the world thirsts for clarity and meaning.[2]

Although it might never have been comfortable for clergy to define what they offered as a product during the modern industrial age, they benefitted from the cultural ethos it shaped, where leaders were in charge. Today, there is no clear path because being "in charge" is no longer assumed or embraced. Leaders must work together with the community not only to move in a direction but first to define one, with many voices—rather than just the voice of the one holding power over resources—competing for influence. Communities find themselves free to maneuver in many different directions, but that freedom is not always a relief to leaders, whose roles become less clear with each new criterion introduced for evaluating their performance. In short, the world is more complicated for leaders now than it was three or four generations ago, and they need more preparation and support. In transitional times, leaders must pull their communities back in two directions. They must prevent their constituents from rushing ahead with false certainty, driven by discomfort with uncertainty. At the same time, they must stop their communities from falling back on old ways due to the same anxiety. People look to their leaders for clarity, yet the leader must keep the community together and functioning as a new identity—and God's will for the community—takes shape.[3]

Leaders and those they lead require a new form of simplicity that emerges from complexity, borrowing an aphorism from Oliver Wendell Holmes Sr., who famously wrote in a letter to Sir Frederick Pollock: "The only simplicity for which I would give a straw is that which is on the other side of the complex—not that which never has divined it."[4] The simplicity needed today cannot replicate yesterday's top-down hierarchies, which endured only because of communities' craving for straightforward solutions in an overwhelming world. Culture-wide desire for simplicity will find satisfaction, one way or another. Ideally, communities will appoint and support leaders who present pathways forward that are clear, understandable, and achievable. If authoritarianism is the only available option to feed their hunger for simplicity, however, that is what they will choose.

The way leaders lead is, as a matter of course, a continuation of how they were developed as leaders. Therefore, leaders who were trained using clear, understandable, and achievable methods are more likely to embody those traits. Furthermore, the way they learn to lead can—and should—be the first chapter of a pattern of lifelong learning for leadership. The leader who charts pathways for continuous growth for their organizations and themselves will find that all are growing together, even if the leader and the organization part ways at some point. Leaders and organizations need plans and pathways now more than ever amid competing demands and definitions of success.

Intentional plans for ongoing leadership development also assist in forming leaders in less-established ministry settings, particularly those who have had less access to educational resources and mentoring. In this way, simple leadership development frameworks are a matter of social justice. Mentors and leadership development programs are far more accessible to those with time, money, and connections—all of which are resources held by the few.

Perhaps the greatest failing of higher education in the US has been its evolution toward elitism. Attempts to expand access encounter resistance, and those with the least power often pay the price for barriers to entry, such as higher education debt and educational programs that make managing competing commitments—such as paid work and family life—exhausting or impossible. Although those from disadvantaged backgrounds may have more access to education than they once did, the cultural attitude that leadership development and other forms of learning are luxuries that one must be able to afford remains unchallenged and highly influential. Leadership development commitments must be simple and adaptable to fit into lives that have no room for them, as only the most elite have been encouraged to prioritize postgraduate learning aimed at growth in effectiveness.

A second social justice implication of a simplified framework for leadership development relates to the nature of complexity in the academy. Only those with time and money have space in their working lives for that which is overly time-consuming. Therefore, intellectual elites protect their positions by excluding from conversation anyone who lacks time to spare. Those elites need not fear and need not overcomplicate what could be simpler, as adopting a manageable theoretical framework for pursuing a self-directed or school-provided curriculum for leadership development can provide tremendous relief for everyone. In fact, a heady intellectual who cannot explain their ideas simply and understandably is not likely as fluent in those ideas as they appear.

The Christian church, as it is known in North America and Europe, is in the process of collapsing and has partially collapsed already. Goal orientation in the absence of a clear, shared vision for the future is bound to discourage those who view leadership as goal-chasing and nothing more. Ministerial leaders now function in a setting where everyone suffers both from information overload and from a lack of balanced perspectives, compounded by oversaturation with media input.

Leaders serve communities where members are increasingly different from one another, and those communities are located in settings that are also rapidly diversifying. Such times seem to defy the development of a straightforward theory, rife as they are with complexity. That said, it is precisely in times of overwhelming complexity that a framework becomes most helpful, as it provides a structure for intentionality rather than succumbing to feelings of helplessness. This framework must take into consideration that ministerial leaders are not merely drum majors, leading the marching band from here to there. They also model informed thinking, theological depth, and openness to what God is doing now. All these leadership practices can be taught, can be learned, and can be improved upon over the course of a lifetime in ministry.

The following illustration highlights the disconnect between providing leadership amidst uncertainty and offering leadership that is simply vague and ambiguous.

An organization that supports religious leaders at every phase of career development invited me as a participant observer to an event they hosted. This organization offered a program for those trained as scholars of religion to explore careers in my field, theological educational administration, and the event was an opportunity for participants to share what they had learned.

By way of background, here is why this leadership development program was important: Most people who have earned PhDs in religion pursued that path with the hope of teaching and writing within the context of the academy. Such roles are increasingly hard to come by, but high-level training in religion provides familiarity with the field and critical thinking skills that have other applications. Educational administrators in theology and religion design curricula, interpret trends in scholarship so theological schools might meet and advance them, and strategize about turning ideas into realities. I was honored to bear witness to this organization's work as it endeavors to expand graduates' thinking about their options and prepare them for leadership.

The presentations were optimistic, insightful, and painted my field in a good light. That was a refreshing change, in that many with PhDs in religion have been trained by their professorial advisors to think of administration as a purgatorial waste of time. Those given the impression by those they seek to imitate that administration is the landing place for those who could not get "real" jobs in the academy are often oblivious to how that impression has shaped their view of educational leadership as a bother. Not only does such modeling form faculty members with whom deans find it difficult to work, but it also undermines needed efforts on the part of today's PhD candidates to investigate relevant alternatives to the disappearing tenure track. During and after presentations, I offered words of hearty congratulations and felt honored myself, as these graduate students treated me like my path through educational administration was one they found inspiring.

As presentations came to a close, participants shared some of their experiences in applying for jobs in administration. The one who spoke first told the story of being asked the typical, yet impossible, question in an interview: "What is your vision for our school?" Anyone who has been asked that question as an external candidate can tell you how delicate it is. No one wants to come across as so arrogant as to think they could come in from the outside and tell an organization what it is and where it should go. Even worse for the internal candidate, answering the question in a way that suggests change is needed risks implying that current leaders—their own administrator colleagues—are not doing a good job.

The participant who spoke said he answered the question with all humility. He told the search committee he had no idea. He came away with the impression that the committee thought his answer was exactly right. Participants in the workshop laughed in what seemed to me an admiring fashion, to the point where I felt compelled to break through the participant-observer fourth wall. I said I could understand why that question felt like a trick, and I agreed that no candidate could know the answer to it. But I made it known to the rest of the group that they should never ever answer an interview question like that in the future. Whether it "worked" for this candidate or not, I never found out, as I do not know if he got the job. But I do know that candidates have to come across as competent and tenacious. "I don't know" is not even an answer my eighth-grade algebra teacher would have accepted.

Instead, I advised the group that they should describe *the process* they would use to work with the community to discern a vision and plot a path together toward achieving it. Pretend, I told them, that they had been asked these questions: *How would you work with the community to formulate a vision? What values, and what style, would you bring to that process? On what data would you rely, and how would you map out the steps between a vision that was nebulous or nonexistent to one that was clear, compelling, and shared?*

Leaders today cannot describe the future with utter confidence, but communities still need to have confidence in them. They need to demonstrate that they are capable of leading in an in-between-eras cultural moment that is disrupting institutions. Why? Because we need these institutions to hold together long enough to get us to a clearer and more legible cultural moment where we know what needs to change and can change it.

The Trefoil Model

A developing ministerial leader grows in multiple directions, not in one direction from point A to point B or from the bottom to the top of a ladder. Leadership development requires growth inward

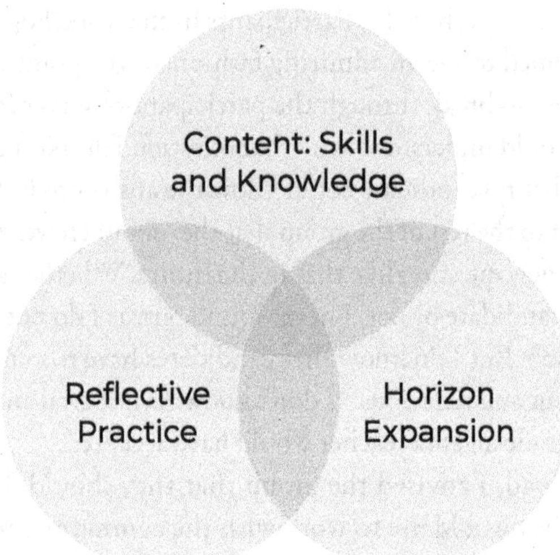

Figure 3.1.

in self-knowledge, outward in the expanding appreciation of the complexity and diversity of creation, and beyond one's comfort zone to become more competent in leading others through knowledge and skills.

The trefoil shape in Figure 3.1 suggests that while the center—like in a Venn diagram—remains the focal point for efforts in leadership development, the true goals should be achieving balance. Many people believe that formal leadership development is not necessary for them, and they are not necessarily wrong. But when examining the choices of those who are indeed effective leaders, one is likely to find that they are engaging in balanced efforts that reflect the priorities of learning content, reflecting on their practice, and exposing themselves to new ways of thinking. Whether intentional or accidental, these three types of activity foster personal and leadership growth. The trefoil model thus represents not just the areas of ministerial leadership development to which leaders must attend, but also the balanced coordination of their attention among them.

The first dimension of the trefoil is: *Know your stuff.* A ministerial leader must engage in intellectual pursuits that provide them with the raw material, in the form of knowledge, that they can integrate into meaning. A minister who does not read, who does not pay attention to culture, and who does not engage in good practices for media literacy runs the risk of passing along half-baked ideas and signaling to others that doing so is acceptable or faithful. Even in an increasingly secular society, communities privilege the words and ideas shared by ministers. That privilege comes with responsibility.

The second dimension is: *Know yourself.* Leaders across fields suffer when they are not sufficiently grounded in a higher meaning that comes from engagement with that which is transcendent. They must also deepen their self-knowledge so they can be strong enough to face new challenges. Strength comes from recognizing one's triggers and fundamentally knowing oneself as a beloved child of God. Without such grounding in transcendent meaning and self-awareness, leaders are likely to panic when faced with the unforeseen and respond in the way others demand, rather than by doing what is right. Some leaders possess strong, ethical, core principles from their first day on the job, but most must develop those principles through examining their lived experiences and engaging in meaningful theological reflection on what they do every day.

The third dimension is: *Know you do not know it all, and keep on growing.* Ministerial leadership comes with discomfort. Most who pursue communal leadership as a profession do so because they like and care about people, yet being disliked by some is one of the costs of ministry. Functioning effectively in such settings requires more than a thick skin and confidence. Leading amid diversity and with openness calls upon leaders to broaden their horizons regularly, stretching their capacities for discomfort in the interest of deepening their understanding of how the world works—and where it doesn't. Practices that broaden a leader's horizons help cultivate a nonjudgmental, compassionate perspective on others and, crucially, toward oneself.

No single leadership development practice will suffice in this season of rapid cultural change. Leadership is too complicated, and it is too hard. Just as a ladder is prone to collapse, leadership growth that depends on a monolithic, linear concept of progress is too risky psychologically. Just as a "great man" is likely to be found to have feet of clay, pursuing leadership development through mimicking someone successful might enable a person to "fake it until they make it," but it will not lead to substantive inner growth. Inner growth and an expanded perspective must accompany solid, foundational knowledge and a commitment to continually improving one's skills.

The Mentality to Which the Trefoil Model Aspires

What are the hoped-for outcomes of a leadership development theoretical framework? Of course, the ideal toward which the one who develops leaders strives is that the institution will be served by wise stakeholders who are capable of carrying out the institution's mission. Yet one could define the ideal of a developed leader in so many, different ways that a higher level of specificity is in order.

In French culture and conversation, the term *mentalité* appears frequently. The American *mentalité* is understood to differ from the French one, and contrasting *mentalités* account for disagreements among political parties and tendencies associated with different generations. The English word *attitude* does not capture the fixedness inherent in a person's mentality. An attitude can change quickly by choice, whereas a mentality takes shape over time and within a specific context. It is easy to tell someone to change their attitude, but altering a mentality is much harder, and sustaining that new mentality requires constant attention. Therefore, defining the mentality leaders need—and must sustain—to be effective in an in-between season is important and cannot be taken for granted. The one described below can be understood as both the goal of the trefoil model and the foundation upon which such a model can be most effectively built.

The trefoil model strives toward a sustainable leadership practice that avoids extremes and nurtures leaders capable of confronting the most overwhelming challenges of the day. One way to frame the trefoil model's goal is to develop leaders who can embody both *wonder* and *wherewithal.* Wonder shapes leaders who are not angry or frustrated when their work becomes challenging, but rather view the underlying sources of difficulties with curiosity and consider them fascinating. Wherewithal is the capacity to stick with seemingly unresolvable questions for as long as the situation demands. The opposing tendences to wonder and wherewithal—easy answers and abdication—should be avoided.

Wonder Versus Answers

When it comes to leaders' comportment and predisposition, *wonder* is a preferred affect to *answers* during times of rapid change. Effective leaders today must remain curious, for there is so much that neither they nor those in their care do not know about the present and the future. A leader's curiosity signals that they are willing to listen to others and take their views seriously—especially when those individuals possess knowledge that the leader does not. An attitude of wonder conveys confidence, as a leader who responds to new information with fascination rather than fear appears assured in their ability to handle whatever they might discover. Such a leader approaches new challenges as opportunities for learning and growth rather than as threats.

Sustaining wonder requires both good mental health and the capacity to accept that they may disappoint people. When a leader is exhausted, depressed, or discouraged, curiosity is hard to summon. A leader might also avoid learning about certain problems because they fear encountering something they cannot fix, thus disappointing those who bring these issues to light. A lack of curiosity does not always indicate a disinterest in learning. It more typically reflects a leader's inability to absorb any more bad news because they are feeling overwhelmed or would rather not know about what they cannot fix.

Leading with *wonder* stands in contrast to a leader who is quick to provide *answers.* Although those in the leader's care might think they want immediate answers, leaders who skip over wonder and rush to answers often do so either out of arrogance or insecurity. The arrogant leader assumes they have seen everything before and have ready-made diagnoses at hand. Such a leader sees no need to delve deeply into the realities experienced by their constituents, as they consider it an unworthy use of their time. Once they arrive at a solution their mental framing, their mental framing of the issue is set in stone, and everyone else must adopt the arrogant leader's interpretation of reality if they want to remain connected with leadership decisions moving forward.

In ministry and other professions whose bottom line is positive human transformation, the arrogant leader is far less common than the desperately insecure one. The results of the oversimplified, knee-jerk reactions of the insecure leader are the same as the results of the arrogant one: engagement through disengaging from real people and their messy, complicated, real problems. An insecure leader seeks to close the gap between questions and answers as quickly as possible, feeling inadequate during times of uncertainty. They fear that too much time in ambiguity will expose their incompetence, leading to a loss of respect. The insecure leader will therefore make premature decisions without fully understanding the situation. In their haste to provide solutions, the gap between the leader and the led community's realities grows larger, and the cost is relevance. Relevance requires attunement, and wonder is the frequency to which relevance is tuned.

Sustaining wonder requires a different kind of discipline than the conventional "getting-things-done" leadership style. Wonder calls for the capacity to balance tensions—attending to the here-and-now with curiosity and unflinching honesty, and hold the needs of individuals without losing sight of those of the broader community. A leader who engages with wonder must also insist on structure while making room for creativity. These tensions serve as a different kind of plumb line for a leader working with insufficient data points to cast a clear vision for the future. A leader cannot manage the anxiety of in-between times without some mental model for staying present amid uncertainty.

Ministerial leaders draw from the well of theology, just as doctors draw from biological sciences and lawyers draw from the law.

Theology—God-knowledge—offers tremendous depth, breadth, and resources. It is neither arbitrary nor unknowable, but it resists being compressed into easy answers. To simplify theology into soundbites and aphorisms risks ruining what makes it compelling in the first place: the recognition that much of God-knowledge is inherently unattainable. Religious know-it-alls embarrass themselves when they pretend to dispense perfect information, for only God's mind is truly unknowable—for only God is God—and looking through the lens of love for truth is an inexact science.

Ministers of all kinds can never be perfectly certain that they are following God to God's specifications, and this uncertainty compounds as new moral questions emerge and challenge leaders. It was never fair to expect ministerial leaders to have answers to life's most difficult questions, and now that expectation is outright impossible. Yet ministers continue to feel pressure to pretend they have those answers. Ministry has always been difficult, but those difficulties are amplified by complexity. The challenges of ministerial leadership are therefore expanding exponentially. Ministry is not the only profession upon which society places unrealistic expectations for all-knowingness. The leaders that should concern their constituents most are those who believe that their followers are right to trust them to resolve every problem and answer every question.

Expectations—especially tacit ones—often cause leaders to fail, appear to fail, or feel like they have failed. Human resources are finite, and no amount of training can prepare a minister to answer questions about the unknowable. The expectation that leaders must have all the answers should have changed generations ago, and now its futility has been laid bare by the scope and scale of cultural change in the early twenty-first century.

Wherewithal Versus Abdication

Abdication, whether in the form of resignation or emotional withdrawal, is a natural temptation for a leader, and sometimes it is exactly what should happen. The leader may choose to resign and pursue a different kind of challenge where success seems more attainable, thereby safeguarding their mental health. Alternatively, the leader might step back from a contentious situation to preserve their stamina for future efforts. Although such actions might benefit the individual, they can harm institutions if they occur too frequently or for prolonged periods. Formal resignations lead to constant turnover and a loss of experience and institutional memory. "Resignation-in-place"—where a leader disengages without formally stepping down—creates a vacuum where others, lacking the necessary authority, do what needs to be done and find themselves constantly out on a limb. Stagnation sets in not just for the leader, but for the community, and those who were forced into positions where they had to make decisions for which they were not authorized become obvious candidates for scapegoating.

Wherewithal, by contrast, is a preferred state of being. It suggests dogged determination and perseverance that help institutions press forward even through stormy periods. A leader with wherewithal sustains a sense of wonder over time, making decisions with due deliberation and openness to feedback, even when it is difficult to hear. Such a leader does not simply push through problems without regard for their own well-being; instead, they rest when necessary, or pause to let solutions take shape. They avoid reaching the point of exhaustion or frustration where disengagement becomes inevitable. When knocked down, they rise again—not aggressively, but with curiosity about what brought them down and with a mindset oriented toward learning rather than retaliation.

Leading with wonder and wherewithal is more of an art than a science, but it is an approach that can be refined over time. In *Composing a Life*, Mary Catherine Bateson advises leaders to take their cues from quilting and jazz,[5] drawing on different forms of knowledge and experience and allowing them to interact in innovative ways. Bateson's approach emphasizes improvisation, collection, and experimentation, which enable leaders to create something new and adaptable for unprecedented, transitional periods.

In adult learning theory, there are two main stances an educational opportunity might adopt: "behaviorist" or "constructivist."

Behaviorist education aims to impart knowledge or skills, focusing on specific behavioral changes. Constructivist approaches, by contrast, stress learning how to learn—constructing a more complex worldview by synthesizing diverse experiences and information. When a leader abdicates responsibility because they lack answers, it is often because they believe that problems must be met with solutions. Constructivist approaches, however, encourage leaders to work with their communities to navigate the unknown, co-developing solutions even when definitive answers are not immediately available.

Learning leadership through new content, such as reading books and attending conferences, is a tried-and-true approach on which many rely. Offering opportunities such as courses on leadership and events centered on leadership development is important but sends a wrong signal that leaders are supposed to have all the answers, and that leaders' most important function is sharing those answers. In reality, the more important leadership function is helping a community to figure out how it will together solve its problems, not solving those problems for the community.

For example, educators in many professions face immense pressure to teach students about the latest technological applications. But if history is any guide, today's technology will be outdated by the time students graduate. Educators who do not prioritize teaching such skills are often deemed irrelevant and out of touch. Yet, if leading with wonder is the opposite of leading with answers, leadership development opportunities that emphasize transmission of information send a misleading message, as so many focus on behaviorist transmission of content.

Similarly, leadership learning that considers abdication to be the best approach amid overwhelm sends the wrong message to communities. Leaders do not become less overwhelmed by shirking their duties, nor do they become happier by pulling away from those in their care. A leader who becomes detached in the name of objectivity and clarity risks cutting themselves off from the very most rewarding part of leadership: relationships. These relationships not only make leaders effective, but they also provide satisfaction. Even the renowned teacher of healthy boundaries in leadership, Rabbi Edwin Friedman, emphasized the importance of maintaining a stance of separate-yet-together wholeness:[6] separate, in that good leaders avoid emotional fusion with their communities; together, in that the leader must stay connected with the community, and a healthy boundary is what makes such connection possible. Good leadership education focuses the leader on prioritizing the important over what feels urgent but is not important, living with disappointing people at times, and cultivating practices that remind the leader of who they are and the limitations on their spheres of influence.

Abdication can take many forms. Quitting a job is the most obvious. "Resigning-in-place" is a newer trend made possible by remote work, where supervisors and peers cannot monitor activity, and employees find distractions to avoid full engagement. Other forms of emotional distancing are more subtle, such as a cynical attitude that deflects responsibility by blaming the environment or others. In *Never Call Them Jerks: Healthy Responses to Difficult Behavior,*[7] Arthur Boers offers strategies for staying engaged when faced with challengers. Maintaining engagement is good for leadership and relationships. Distancing oneself due to frustration with others can lead to self-isolation. Leaders may feel pushed away by those who frustrate them, but pushing back usually results in further isolation.

Leaders need to remain engaged with their communities, contexts, and responsibilities in order to have an impact on those they lead and on the wider world. The most basic form of wherewithal—showing up—remains, alongside wonder, key to leadership in an overwhelming and quickly changing era. Attending meetings and events, appearing in hallways and neighborhoods, visiting homes and hospitals: These simple habits cultivate a sense of connection that a leader can draw upon when times are tough. Such practices, though minimal, can have a positive effect on a leader's capacity to stay engaged.

Crises in community life are inevitable. While some can be avoided, many arise unexpectedly and force communities to ask difficult questions and make tough decisions. When a leader has been connected and present, engaging the community during crises is not easy, but it is less traumatic. Regular contact builds trust, and showing up tells the community that the leader is invested and will not make harmful decisions out of uninformed unfamiliarity with what matters most to people. Wonder helps the leader to gather real stories in real time, while wherewithal keeps them engaged in the face of challenges. When crises occur in a relational atmosphere of wonder and wherewithal, communities are more likely to respond with curiosity rather than fear, and to roll up their sleeves together rather than waiting for their leader to swoop in with easy solutions.

The Trefoil Model's Functions

The trefoil model of leadership development serves four practical purposes:

1. Designing a leadership development program from the ground-up
2. Diagnosing why a leadership development protocol is not working
3. Assessing a leader's effectiveness
4. Designing a plan for lifelong leadership learning

Implication for Practice 1: Aiding in Program Design

January 2023

As I write this paragraph, I am in Peru, volunteering at a children's home with my daughter who herself spent her early months in a children's home. We are serving under the leadership of two missionaries, one who has been in Peru his entire life—his parents, too, were missionaries—and one who married into mission work in her late teens. "John's" parents founded a church in one part of the country, and John and "Cora" founded this children's home, as well as the church connected to it.

John received a manual on how to "do" missionary work provided by the umbrella organization that networks missions of this kind together. He knows he must take into consideration the leadership culture of this region, which presents numerous challenges. Peruvian leadership is top-down, influenced by several factors. These include the historic dominance of Roman Catholic Christianity in Peru, with its hierarchical understanding of the ministry of the laity; Peru's recent history of political imperialism and colonialism; resistance to peer-to-peer collaboration that might result in mutual correction (for only the chief has permission to critique); a collective, culture-wide low self-esteem regarding the strength and potential of Peru and of Peruvians; and internalized racism that projects competence and trustworthiness onto those who are whiter in complexion and more European in affectation.

John wants to develop a leadership culture where leadership is shared and responsibility is distributed. While Jesus did not lead by democracy, he used deputization and dissemination of ministry and message. Cora reports that the community surrounding the children's home and church expects her and John to do everything, since they are the missionaries, after all. The community assumes John and Cora have all the answers and nothing else to do but run the church and children's home. Cora realizes that removing opportunities to minister is counterproductive to the health of the community; furthermore, she already carries as much responsibility as one person can manage.

John has learned much through his lifetime of service, and he is now at a point where both he and Cora need fresh perspectives and new ideas to energize lay leaders and encourage them to take on meaningful ministry. They want new colors for their palette, tools and techniques they can incorporate into their leadership practices, expanding their range of options. They invited me to bring a fresh perspective, recognizing that my knowledge of their daily work is superficial and new.

New leadership challenges require moments of truth, when leaders look up and around and realize they need to expand their thinking and options. John and Cora are at that point as they begin to consider who might carry on their mission in the future. They do not want their community to suffer from "founder's syndrome," the pattern where organizations falter after a strong founder departs. Nor do they want the ministry to continue in its current mode, where the missionaries are expected to know and do everything. They want a healthy succession to follow their service.

Cora and John want to build up leaders who have low regard for their own potential. Since they are trying to do something countercultural, they will need non-native materials to build the structure they envision. Much like planting non-native vegetation, they need to proceed with care. Already, new and potentially harmful ideas are flowing into the country through the rapid proliferation of access to technology. Good ideas flow too, of course, but at an unchecked rate. They know better than to repeat the pattern of importing foreign thinking and expecting that what has worked elsewhere will work there.

Over the years they have served as missionaries in Peru, John and Cora have discovered that countercultural work takes time. To motivate people to do something new, leaders must first build trust. If they want to change people's thinking, they must apply constant pressure through repetition, teaching, and patient reintroduction of concepts that do not initially resonate. John is confident that he has taught the Bible faithfully. Now, he needs to bring the same consistent attention to Christian leadership development. The gap between biblical knowledge and leadership is not an unbreachable chasm, but expecting people new to the faith to intuit the implications of biblical knowledge for leadership might be a step too far.

John and Cora have numerous options to consider when designing a leadership development strategy for their ministry. The trefoil model not only provides guidance for developing a strategy but also serves as a reminder that a single intervention—no matter how extensive—will not be enough to bringing about lasting transformation in their community.

When it comes to instilling knowledge in the leaders he seeks to cultivate, John can start with an area where he is already confident: Bible study. He can build upon this foundation by adding leadership themes to his Bible instruction. A close reading of Acts, or a deep dive into Paul's letters, could provide numerous opportunities to transmit new content about the hows, whys, and challenges of leadership. By repeatedly suggesting to his students through Bible study that they—and not just he and Cora—are inheritors of Jesus's mandate to make disciples, they will begin to see themselves in the stories and adopt practices for leadership.

John and Cora can also integrate reflective practices into their ministry by adding weekly debriefs to any activities led by members of the community. John attests that criticism among peers is not part of Peruvian culture, but perhaps evaluating what has and has not worked in events led by various community leaders could feel less personal or invasive. Another option might be to foster feedback solely in the form of affirmations, which can be just as powerful as critique without raising anyone's defenses. Knowing in advance that they will be sharing affirmations can prompt those experiencing leadership to step outside themselves as observers, deepening their self-awareness and building their confidence.

Finally, these missionaries can encourage opportunities for members of their community to observe other leaders in other settings. Whereas Cora and John have served in a variety of mission posts, many of those they minister to have not. Worshiping with another faith community in some sort of exchange could broaden horizons and make more space for creative ideas. Nothing sparks imagination better than witnessing firsthand how different communities interpret their missions in ways that are both diverse and equally faithful. Seeing the multiplicity of potential expressions of the Christian faith can inspire new thoughts and liberate those who feel that only one approach can work.

John and Cora operate from a manual provided by their sponsoring organization on how to conduct their ministries. They could adapt the trefoil leadership development model to their setting without fundamentally altering that manual, as these leadership development practices are designed to be supplemental, broadening learning beyond transmission and toward integration. They might even consider sharing that addendum back with the organization that produces their training manuals, offering it as a new resource that encourages missionaries not just to partner with and uplift coworkers indigenous to their mission settings, but to give them specific guidance on how such leadership development can be done. In a complex, overwhelming, and diverse world, "Develop leadership on the ground" is not an obvious or simple instruction, but the trefoil model can serve as a framework for creating a curriculum that fits these contexts.

Implication for Practice 2: Diagnosing Why a Leadership Development Protocol Is Not Working

For many years, I co-taught a class for theological field education supervisors. A few years into this experience, one participant—who was working with one of my school's master of divinity students as his intern—became aggravated that I and my co-instructor placed such a heavy emphasis on reflective practice. He believed that his role as a supervisor was to teach his students how to complete tasks and that the skills required to carry out those tasks were beyond question. Preach like this, pray like that—he believed he should explain correct practices to his student and be done with it.

When I and others in the class raised the possibility that authentic ministry could not result from merely following paint-by-number instructions, he walked out of the class, never to return. We had to find his student a new supervisor, as the training component was a requirement he refused to fulfill. Ultimately, just a year or two later, his ministry faltered because his prescriptive style was off-putting to leaders who wanted to engage and consult. I, however, came to realize that our course was overemphasizing reflective practice, when skills matter too, and I adapted my instruction in other courses, specifically around instruction on practices for leadership. If this participant had not become so aggravated that he could not stay in the class, he might have noticed a change based on his feedback that he was not getting a balanced perspective.

The illustration above demonstrates that conflict can arise when a leader's understanding of what is required of them is challenged by someone with authority. It tells the story of a person who thinks that leadership development and information transmission about leadership are the same thing, when in reality, task completion is insufficient for true leadership. Teaching only skills, without fostering new ways of thinking, cannot prepare leaders for an unpredictable future.

Most professionals learn about leadership on the job, yet professionals cannot bank decades of experience before making difficult choices that affect their communities. A trefoil approach makes possible the development of a leader without the benefit of the many years' worth of experience required to learn that content, theological reflection, and horizon-expansion all come together to deepen and to expand a leader and that leader's ministry, and they do so quickly in that the three practices shape not just skills, but character.

The second part of the illustration—when the course participant left the class abruptly—could have ended with the author and course instructor shutting down to criticism. His reactive behavior would have made dismissing his concerns easy, and the lesson for the teaching team did not become clear right away. With time and—ironically—reflection, defensiveness gave way to curiosity. An *ad hominem* attack on the dissatisfied course participant might have been expected or even justified, but approaching the incident with wonder and wherewithal transformed it from mere drama into a lesson.

Implication for Practice 3: The Trefoil as an Assessment Tool

An institution, facing serious financial and mission-related challenges that required significant rethinking, hired "Tom" as its CEO. Tom secured the job by promising to inspire innovative thinking and lead the institution in a new direction. His charisma, likability, and previous experience in change management convinced the search committee and board that he could turn the institution around. I worked for Tom.

What I discovered was that Tom was extremely persuasive when delivering his message that everyone needed to think differently, but he did not have clear guidance to offer on what form change should take. He became frustrated easily with conventional problems, but those problems would not resolve themselves, so I and my colleagues needed to tend to them. Unless what we were doing was a meaningful innovation, he did not want to talk, or later even hear, about it, yet inattention to the day-to-day was not acceptable either.

Ultimately, his promises to upend the status quo proved insufficient in and of itself. No major institutional shifts came to pass during Tom's season of leadership.

This third illustration demonstrates that while broadening horizons is necessary for change—since it disrupts tired and unhelpful patterns—when it is not combined with soul-searching and actionable ideas, a focus on change for its own sake lacks substance. The motivational posters one sees on the walls of entrepreneurs' offices may depict exciting images of freestyle mountain climbers dangling from cliffs, but the inspiration they offer to take risks and disrupt staid habits must be followed by deep inner work and enriched by know-how.

Leaders and managers must keep their organizations running smoothly while innovating. They must have the knowledge of their fields and themselves to sustain activity in the present, and continue it during transitional periods, while looking toward the future. Anyone assessing Tom's leadership progress would be well served to ensure that he was knowledgeable about what the community needed to maintain itself, even if everyone agreed that the status quo was not viable long-term. Such evaluators might ask how Tom grounding himself and listening to the institution's immediate needs, even though he was hired to look for new directions. Some might say that expecting a leader to be both a visionary and a competent manager is too much to ask, but this dual-level competence is precisely what institutions need today.

Implication for Practice 4: The Trefoil as a Guide for Lifelong Leadership Learning

I made it through three years of divinity school, including internships and part-time jobs, without realizing that leadership is an area of academic study. I had been told through what educators call the "null curriculum"—sending a message on what is and is not important through what is and is not taught—that leadership was not part of ministry. Upon reading a book about leadership for the first time, after I graduated from divinity school, I felt I had been duped. Five years later, I entered a PhD program on leadership, and that is the area in which I now write and teach.

Still, in many, if not most, graduate theological schools, students learn leadership only through theological reflection rather than receiving instruction on leadership or being engaged in disorienting, yet mind-expanding, learning experiences. Reflecting on internship experiences is incredibly important, but it does not constitute all that future leaders require by way of knowledge. I believe that they must learn how to conduct themselves as leaders, with all relevant skills included, to provide a basic foundation. They also must learn how to decenter themselves and their prior knowledge to make space for new perspectives as new challenges come their way.

The program I lead today requires leadership learning through courses in a school of management, reflective practice in internships, and encounters with new settings that expand horizons. In my own leadership development, I read books, reflect through writing and discussions with colleagues, and seek out experiences that take me outside my comfort zone. I do this despite having had to learn through trial and error what a lifelong practice of ministerial leadership education requires.

Leaders must take responsibility for their own leadership development curricula. Their supervisors or boards might ask them how they are growing, but ultimately only the leader can know what knowledge, reflection, and horizon-broadening practices might look like. A trefoil approach alleviates some of the pressure by providing guidance and the all-important balance that leaders need, given that they can dedicate only a limited amount of time to self-development. A modest, yet trefoil-balanced, self-directed program for leadership growth can be just as transformative as a full degree program in leadership. As adrienne maree brown observes when commenting on fractals—geometrical shapes that remain fundamentally the same regardless of scale[8]—a small but intentional approach to balanced leadership development can become a habit that, over time, shapes a leader's entire life.

Raw Materials

One question one cannot avoid when discussing ministerial leadership is whether talent is relevant or essential. Consider the philanthropic initiatives by major foundations, such as the Lilly Endowment, Inc., which have invested heavily in encouraging intelligent and capable young people to consider ministry as a career path and have generously supported their theological educations and the institutions that provide it. Underlying these efforts is the expectation that the future of ministerial leadership is only as bright as the people who choose to pursue their callings from God and enter the field.

Similarly, many who write about leadership stress the importance of building teams composed of the "right" people. Leaders must consider numerous factors when forming such teams, including who will be respected enough to influence others through their modeling and example, and whether to include dissenters who can sharpen the coalition's focus and ensure that all concerns are addressed. However, leaders must look beyond optics and identity and select only those who are strong collaborators, approaching the work with wonder and determination. In other words, leaders should ask whether a prospective team member has the capacity to work with others in a specific leadership mindset.

Sometimes leaders who possess such a mentality are not available for recruitment. Consider again the example of John (see "Implication for Practice 1"), who sought to develop leaders capable of collaboration and initiative in a postcolonial context. He summarizes his greatest challenge as a dearth of critical thinking skills among the general population he serves. John strives to convey to his community that they must adapt to never-before-seen challenges and create something that has never existed. Yet, the community looks to him for black-and-white instructions. He seeks to inspire imagination for what God can make possible through a community, and that same community asks for "answers." Can critical thinking be taught? Yes, but would leadership development not be so much simpler without having to do so? Absolutely. John found himself in a cultural situation where leaders demonstrating wonder and wherewithal, ready to take on a trefoil approach to leadership development, needed to be homegrown.

Theological educators will happily share stories of students who have transformed dramatically over the course of their studies. They also recount instances where they smiled and applauded as a student walked across the stage to receive a degree that would pave the way for ordination, all the while suppressing deep concerns about the student's character or potential. The Christian faith avoids using terms like "never" when considering the possibilities for human transformation. If resurrection is central to the Christian narrative, how can one justify judging whether a person can ever change? On the one hand, those called to ministerial service must be given every opportunity to succeed and provided with the best preparation and education possible. On the other hand, communities of all kinds deserve the best when it comes to leadership. Subjecting them to an individual who lacks competence or sound judgment is counterproductive for everyone (faith communities) and everything (ultimately, the Gospel) involved.

Ministerial leadership development enables those with natural gifts for leadership to improve and continue to grow as times change, but no leader can declare themselves finished with learning and expect to thrive in quickly changing times. Consider how white, straight, male, cisgender, mainline Protestant ministers have been subject to levels of scrutiny in recent years regarding their ability to understand issues like racism and sexism. In response to movements like Black Lives Matter and Me Too, they must be especially mindful of what they say. Those who are capable of deep inner work are faring far better than those who were trained for ministry and then rested on their laurels. A male-bodied leader who commits to learning about racism and sexism, reflecting deeply on his past experiences and attitudes, and building relationships across differences to broaden his knowledge, has a greater chance of success than his defensive or resentful counterparts. His approach begins with a mentality and leads to action.

Can the leadership development practices described in this book "fix" a person who is not well suited to leadership? That question cannot be answered simply or linearly, as people are not problems to be solved. However, the trefoil model can provide a leader with renewed hope, especially when leadership feels overwhelming, or when they are told they cannot succeed. When leaders feel overwhelmed, they need manageable sets of actions that can set them on a new path. A message suggesting that leaders are either born capable or can never become so is counterproductive in the extreme.

Ministerial leadership today is, as has been reiterated in various ways, difficult and increasingly complex. In their daily work, ministers face issues that none before them have encountered. In the face of the new and unfamiliar, they have choices: They can forge ahead and try to solve problems, or they can ask whether they themselves might be part of the problem and work on self-improvement. Most leaders need to do a little bit of both in order to get through the day. All require more support to grow in ministerial leadership competence than was previously necessary, and that is not to be pathologized but rather accepted as a recognition of today's complex realities. The three-part model for lifelong leadership learning proposed in the trefoil theoretical framework for ministerial leadership development offers a guide for laying out a leadership development program that transcends settings, cultures, and specific circumstances. It has multiple, straightforward applications in this era of overwhelm.

Conclusion

The Christian movement looks to Jesus's death and resurrection for guidance on what he wanted his followers to do after he was gone. One reasonable interpretation of the Gospel suggests that Jesus appointed Peter as his successor. Another view proposes that Jesus appointed no earthly successor at all, instead sending the Holy Spirit for the disciples to share across the world. These diverging understandings of Jesus's succession plan have profound implications for how Christians perceive the roles of their leaders. Yet, whether ministers are understood as descendants of Peter or sharers of the Spirit, both frameworks call upon leaders to grow over the course of their lifetimes and to foster growth in others.

If ministers are like Peter, they must lead their communities as they believe Jesus would have them do. They must acquire knowledge to teach, reflect so they can invite God to illuminate areas for improvement, and step outside their comfort zones to welcome the world's wonder into their practices. If they are called upon to share the good news and enliven the Holy Spirit in those in their care, the same principles—acquiring knowledge, reflecting, and expanding horizons—apply, but with an emphasis on encouragement, authorization, and empowerment for others first.

Whichever framework is embraced, both require lifelong growth in the leaders themselves and an ongoing commitment to empowering the leaders around them. Peter may have been a chief cornerstone, but he was not meant to work alone. The Holy Spirit, too, was a gift meant to create connections within communities, connections that require consistent cultivation and care.

CHAPTER FOUR

Leadership Development Through Conveying Knowledge, Information, and Skills

---

A lay leader took me on a tour of his church's beautiful sanctuary. Outside, an entire city block was under construction. He invited me to look through a small opening in the plywood to see the gigantic building project underway—a project that had nearly sunk the church for reasons that broke my heart to hear. The church was the rightful owner of the adjacent city block, including the air rights above it. A developer had made them promises of a perpetual income stream if they allowed the land to be turned it into high-end condos, and the church's board and staff welcomed the idea.

In the end, through legal maneuvers and financial missteps, the developer went out of business, and the church lost its property and air rights. How could this have happened? The answer lies with a board whose members did not know what they did not know and clergy who did not feel it was their place to insist they do their homework. None of those involved would—or should—have been expected to possess detailed knowledge of real estate finance and law, but feelings of overwhelm and uncertainty about where to start may have kept leaders from taking the necessary steps to understand the implications of their decisions.

Leadership effectiveness requires a significant amount of homework. As a broad term for all that a person can do to grow in their practice of leadership, "professional development" suggests an expansive program. The term "professional" indicates a focus on the leadership demands of a specific field, while "development" suggests that, through a programmatic intervention, the professional not only acquires new information but also experiences growth. Most formal professional development programs across fields are unidimensional, providing the learner with information relevant to their profession and conveying practical skills.

It is therefore surprising when leaders do not take seriously the importance of gathering, synthesizing, and adapting in light of newly emerging content in their fields. Some resist pressures to stay updated because they do not perceive such pressures; they are already treated as experts. Others do not recognize how quickly the world is changing around them and underestimate how much work is needed to stay abreast of trends. Some might not know where to start, feeling overwhelmed by the sheer abundance of content and unable to parse what information is most urgent versus what is most important. Finally, some make the misguided assumption that no one could reasonably expect a leader to know information that is not readily available—especially if that information is outside their professional domain.

Of course, the cost of seeking out and mastering the information one needs to lead effectively is high, and not only, or even primarily, in monetary terms. Learning pertinent information and content for leadership requires a substantial investment of time and demands humility. Time is needed to parse a good question, explore various answers, and integrate new information into what may be deeply ingrained habits. Humility drains energy in a different way, as the leader must face the possibility that they do not know everything, that they might have been doing something they should not to have been doing, or that they may have been *so wrong* for *so long* that some ego healing is necessary.

Leaders may have to face the truth that there are others out there who know more than they ever will about something important, which can prompt an existential crisis. If theologian Paul Tillich had it right, these anxieties all find their origin point in the fear of death,[1] and such anxiety is not unwarranted. After all, no one will live long enough to know even a fraction of everything. The realization that no one can ever know it all can inspire wonder, but the shadow side of that wonder is the impostor syndrome experienced by leaders at their low points.

Followers of leaders do not always encourage a leader's curiosity about what they do not know. Reasonable recipients of leadership do expect that a leader will train up on what must be known, but do not anticipate the leader knowing everything under the sun. In reality, not all followers are reasonable; some prefer demagogues or cult figures who pretend to possess all the answers. Moreover, the embarrassment of being called out on a topic where the leader lacks knowledge does not spark the leader's creativity but instead triggers shame. A healthy, mature leader will respond to questions they cannot answer with, "I am going to need to look into that and get back to you." A less healthy, less mature, or more overwhelmed leader may pretend to know, shut down, or recycle truisms. In these cases, doing more homework and training up on new content will not be the tools to which an overwhelmed leader will reach.

These psychological barriers that dull a leader's drive to really and truly know their field must come down. These barriers affect leaders from diverse fields and settings differently, depending on variations in context and identity. In terms of context, a leader is less likely to feel comfortable admitting they do not know everything if they are a surgeon, since lives are at stake in their field. In contrast, a preacher trying to make spiritual sense of a new social phenomenon might be more at ease with uncertainty. The risks of harm to a client elevate anxieties about not knowing enough or about being "caught" looking something up or asking for advice. As for identity, those who come from groups who have long occupied the corridors of societal power are considered down-to-earth and humble when they acknowledge what they do not know and take the risk of setting out to learn more. In contrast, those whose backgrounds make them newcomers to such corridors face scrutiny, and in the same situations, they feel a very real threat of being excluded or delegitimized.

Some barriers to learning new content can be overcome more easily than others. A discipline of intentional skill- and content-learning gets the leader over the lower barriers first (such as overwhelm), building momentum to confront the more difficult ones (such as fear of irrelevance). Information and skills are crucial for professional effectiveness. As the context in which leaders operate changes, they must stay apprised of innovations and trends. Doing so not only helps them to serve effectively but also sets the stage for other forms of leadership development, such as reflective practice and horizon expansion. As the leader's pool of curiosity grows, it tends to spill over across different areas, fostering growth in multiple directions.

Staying up to date helps leaders refine their work and stokes the desire to learn even more. It also provides the therapeutic benefit of making the leader feel less isolated. When they discover that the challenges they face are common enough to warrant the creation of professional resources, leaders often find solace. For example, if courses exist for leaders working in toxic environments rife with conflict, this must mean that conflict is common, or even normal. Leaders become aware through their search for resources that the patterns affecting them are part of a bigger national or global issue, and they are less likely to blame themselves for finding those problems difficult. Overcoming shame and self-doubt makes them better learners—more curious than afraid that something is wrong with them. Better learners, in turn, become better leaders.

Learning Skills

Indispensable, but Never Enough

Skills-oriented, information-transmitting leadership development education must take place within a broader context of growth and learning. Like money hidden in a mattress rather than invested in an interest-bearing account, skills-based learning becomes less valuable over time due to the inflationary tendency whereby cultural change outpaces the leader's skill set. In the realm of education for professional effectiveness, mentalities about the role of skills-based learning swing between extremes, with one view saying that skills are everything and another claiming that they are bound for obsolescence.

Programs for mid-career professionals that focus on skill-based learning are easy to locate, access, and pursue. Employers and vendors offer training on technologies and information-based approaches to supervising staff. Programs emphasizing reflective practice and horizon expansion, however, are less abundant. Ironically, highly educated professionals often view skills-based learning negatively and approach it with preconceived notions that such programs are a waste of time. The area of leadership development that has the most abundant resources available and easiest access is the one that highly educated, practicing leaders are likely to approach with a closed mind. One hears professionals bemoaning mandatory training on new workforce skills, and employers sometimes package them within luxury vacations to make them more palatable.

Many professional development programs provide learners with opportunities to learn new skills or information and nothing else. They attend to just one dimension of the trefoil leadership education model. The other two dimensions—horizon expansion and reflective practice—take place most commonly outside the context of professional development programming. This reality is not, in and of itself, a problem. Formal interventions that focus on information and skills are useful and immediately practical. However, when not situated within a broader developmental growth program, their effectiveness is limited in several ways, including in the shelf life of new knowledge. Skills-oriented professional learning matters, but without deepening self-knowledge and expanding one's understanding of the wider world, it fades with time.

Professionals whose formation took place in the context of formal, graduate-level education sometimes look askance at skill-building professional development. They attend educational events conveying practical content with arms folded, closed off to the experience. They may resent attending such events when mandated by professional guilds, perceiving practical learning as beneath them, whether they admit it outwardly or not, and that mentality affects the way new information sinks in. Consciously, they learn little. Unconsciously, they develop a negative attitude toward skill-based learning, even when the training addresses emergent needs.

Negative attitudes toward skill development have deep roots in the academy. Ancient Greek hierarchies of knowledge, where the contemplative person was the society's brain and the practical-active person its muscle, still frame academic culture. Even in an era when the liberal arts suffer from declining interest as students gravitate toward majors and graduate degrees that promise higher earnings, the more abstract disciplines continue to receive nearly reverent protection.

The ideal to which educators ought to strive, particularly in preparing learners for professional effectiveness, is strong skills rooted in wisdom, an integration of the practical with the abstract.[2] Such grounding assures that practical skills hold on to their value as leaders pivot in times of change. The conventional assumption that true scholars focus on the abstract, while a trained dog could master a skill the way it does a new trick, will be hard to dispel. Just as extroverts are sometimes labeled as gadflies and introverts as "deep," certain cultural assumptions—harking back to the distinction between contemplatives and laborers—remain entrenched.

Today's graduate theological education is infused with the assumption that the most abstract disciplines are the occupation of the smartest on the faculty and in the student body. Therefore, as a matter of course, the most on-the-ground and least contemplative subjects are relegated to the realm of the less heady and less wise. As a result, those whose self-worth derives in part from their intellectual abilities might not value skill-based learning through information and content-focused instruction. Yet skills, which are outcroppings of deeper wisdom, are important for professional effectiveness. No one learns them through osmosis but rather through education, training, and practice.

Teaching a skill that will work today and into the very near future does not require significant time or attention. Those seeking professional competence yearn for answers to skill-based questions, and educators must indulge that yearning to a point—if for no other reason than to reduce the learner's anxiety. That said, the educator must not entirely slake the learner's thirst, as skills alone will wither absent rootedness in wisdom that results from sustained formation. The following example illustrates the balance an educator must strike between providing sufficient information to satisfy the learner and recognizing that explanation is only a small part of what the learner needs to develop competence.

I like to boast to my students that I can explain to them how to officiate a wedding in under three minutes. I have even asked them to time me. Here is what I tell them:

A couple approaches you and asks you to preside at their wedding. If you can, you say yes, because it is a worthy and honorable thing to do. You meet with them, ask them about their lives and their love, and get to know them. You arrange for two more meetings to talk about marriage with them, where you pose questions about their past, present, and future and let them talk to you while they overhear what the other says. Between sessions, you take the order of worship recommended in your tradition and populate it based on what the couple is telling you about their lives. During a fourth and final meeting, you go over the draft service with them, explaining your choices, and asking them for their input.

You plan a rehearsal for the night before the wedding but you go in with everything already mapped out. You work out a detailed diagram, noting who stands where and who speaks when. If you have never done this before, ask an experienced colleague to help you. If you are presiding in a setting with staff, seek their advice on technical details like sound systems and the logistics of the procession and recessional.

Run the rehearsal like a drill sergeant, putting each participant through their paces while making it clear that this service is a moment of worship and blessing. It can be playful and joyful, but it is not a joke. Later, the couple will thank you for putting the class-clown maid of honor or the self-conscious best man in their best frame of mind. They will ask you to come to the rehearsal dinner, and unless you are their best friend or relative, you politely decline.

On the day of the wedding, arrive early. Introduce yourself to the musicians, coordinate cues, and establish a sense of partnership. Check in with the bride and pray with her—trust me, she needs it. Check in with the groom, and you do the same. Tell them both that something will inevitably go wrong and that mishaps will be an important reminder that this is a ceremony of covenanting, not an opening night on Broadway, and it will make for a great story. Then preside over the service, congratulate the bride and groom, and leave—having already told them that you cannot attend the reception because of other ministry duties the next day.

The factual information in the example above about officiating a wedding requires little instruction for the ministry learner. The more complex dimensions of the illustration relate to theological questions, such as: "What does it mean to say the wedding is a 'worship service'?" "What should be the contents of the prayers? The getting-to-know-you premarital preparation sessions?" or "To what extent is the minister the premarital 'counselor' versus the preparer of a liturgy?" Presiding at weddings is an excellent opportunity to connect with people who may have previously discounted the role faith could play in their lives. Learning the technicalities is easy, but connecting—personally and emotionally—is also important to the couple, their loved ones, and a wider culture seeking a deeper and more meaningful understanding of human relationships.

Attending to the administrative details of presiding at a wedding and knowing how to carry out the minister's responsibilities before and during the ceremony is crucial. Families have expectations for a smooth and satisfying service of worship. Technical knowledge and skill demonstrate the minister's competence, and when the minister is competent, those supporting the couple can relax and become more present in the moment. Even so, technical competence in curating, coordinating, and officiating a wedding ceremony is only one part of conveying trustworthiness and ministerial effectiveness. It is fully realized only when the minister is deeply self-aware and radically open-minded, requiring a broader array of professional formation than skills training alone can provide.

Beyond skills and good habits, the minister needs to understand their own inner life fully so that they do not project their own experiences onto the couple they are serving. The minister must also have enough experience beyond their own circumstances to approach those getting married without presuppositions or judgment. Technical skills do not prepare a minister to help a new family through deep, meaningful questions about what marriage means and what God's role is within it, but these actions and skills are essential to building a safe and sacred space for those who have turned to the minister for support and guidance.

Information- and Skills-Based Learning

Basic formation for professional effectiveness in fields like ministry often begins in graduate school. Universities include many different schools, some of them professional. Education scholars debate whether learning a skill differs fundamentally from learning information or whether the two are essentially one and the same. Traditionally, elite universities have separated information-based instruction and skill-based learning into different parts of the curriculum—such as classroom instruction versus hospital-based clinical rotations in medical education—or excluded skills instruction altogether, as is common in liberal arts education for the humanities. More likely, however, learners become accustomed to bridging theory and practice within siloed graduate programs, ultimately equipping them to continue learning on the job, as integration has been their responsibility all along.

When cultivating lifelong learning for leadership, beyond a first layer of professional education in graduate school, learners seek opportunities to gather information and implement what they have learned. In ministry, this pattern typically plays out when the aspiring professional pursues a master of divinity as a terminal professional degree granted by accredited theological schools. Master of divinity programs include learning about Christian heritage: the Bible, theology, history, and ethics—while attending to the cultural and societal contexts surrounding and influencing that heritage, both now and in the future. These programs provide leadership education through coursework and supervised ministry. To be approved as an accredited master of divinity program, schools must include spiritual formation in both the curriculum and co-curriculum.[3]

For any number of reasons, not all ministers have access to, or interest in attaining, graduate-level education for the purpose of entering ministry. For some, ministry is part of a larger set of vocational aspirations and professional responsibilities, making a three-year master of divinity unrealistically out of proportion with the whole of the minister's life. The time and money required to pursue graduate studies in any discipline is privilege not everyone can enjoy. Because people, congregations, and contexts differ one from the other, a one-size approach to education for ministry does not fit all.

Nevertheless, the standard master of divinity provides guidance for what a theological education for ministry should include. A religious leader in a faith community needs to know more about the Bible than what rests on its pages; they must develop skills for interpreting it carefully and thoughtfully. They need training in exegesis and hermeneutics from someone well versed in biblical scholarship for a ministry that relies on sacred texts for making meaning. Similarly, understanding Christian history and the role of Christianity in culture—both historically and in the present—provides the leader with an essential competency: being able to place today's events within a wider framework. A minister can learn about history and culture through reading, coursework, and careful attention to current events, but in the absence of the intentional devotion of time, they cannot internalize the sheer volume of information required to integrate and apply it to their faith community's situations.

Skills-based learning might be the easiest form of knowledge to obtain on the job. Ministers and other professionals can locate instructions and acquire information without incurring high costs. That said, the human mind and the professional's competence are not enhanced by downloading information. The foundation undergirding skills requires theological and ethical training. For example, a person could preside over a worship service for a specific occasion by reading a ready-made liturgy found online. However, merely reciting a worship service is only the tip of the iceberg for a ministerial leader. Beneath the surface of the liturgy is a living, breathing body of theology that brings words to life. A minister officiating a funeral, for instance, builds their words on a faith that, ultimately, life prevails over death, even if that precise sentiment is not explicitly stated.

Educators reasonably worry that devoting too much time to skills instruction will give learners excuses to master those skills and then stop there. Satisfied with beautiful, cut flowers, they might not plant perennial concepts that will blossom over the course of a lifetime. Educators are wise to worry that suggesting that future professionals can rely solely on skills without a theological foundation may result in ministry malpractice, which risks harming the ministry's recipients. Learning how to perform a skill without understanding its roots in the Christian faith tradition exposes the ministerial leader—and the broader Christian community—to various risks.

A minister who does not understand the meaning behind their tasks is unlikely to convey the depth and richness of the Christian faith to future generations of ministers. Such a leader will be ill-equipped to answer the faith community's questions today and even less prepared to address unforeseen questions that require the weaving together of multiple forms of knowledge. Graduate theological school is just one way to obtain the knowledge that undergirds ministry skills, but no theological education—whether before ministry or ongoing throughout it—risks harm to Christianity as a movement and way of life. Theological schools arose out of concerns for the future of the faith. Although cultural expectations for graduate theological education have changed, concern that future clergy would not have what they need to perpetuate and grow the faith has not gone away.

Beyond formal, degree-granting education, ministers today have a broad array of resources to support lifelong learning. They can access libraries and work with librarians to find books and journals that are peer-reviewed and vetted for quality. They can create a curriculum of reading with the guidance of both librarians and colleagues who are further along in ministry. The vast amount of information available to an aspiring minister is as much a curse as it is a blessing. The blessing of easy access to written materials is one that the early Christian ministers in New England could have hardly imagined. The first ministers in the Colonies learned ministry through an apprenticeship model, where young men would move into ministers' parsonages and assist them. This educational approach arose in part because only ministers had libraries in their homes with the theological books a ministry learner would need.

Today, access to information is easy, but quality control is essential. The challenges associated with ensuring high-quality resources almost negate the value of easy access. Today's internet algorithms are sophisticated enough to provide answers to arcane and specific questions but not sophisticated enough to filter for political stances or uninformed opinions. While it is easy to find facts online, deeper interpretation requires a trained, critical eye. Online discussion forums offer benefits by connecting people around the globe and giving a voice to the previously voiceless. They also provide platforms for people who misuse them—people who wish to recruit others to hateful viewpoints through irresponsible interpretations of scripture and history. Since online platforms provide solace and support as well as misinformation and disinformation, they must not to be ignored or dismissed but should be viewed through the lens of critical thought.

With or without the possibility of a degree at its end, formal educational programs structure learning, guide readers toward deeper thinking, and facilitate the internalization and integration of new knowledge. Books might be the food, but courses can serve as the digestive system, and they are more broadly available now than in the past due to online learning opportunities. Courses within the faith community, such as Bible study and reading groups, offer the added benefit of learning in a community setting. Learning together deepens relationships, thereby enhancing both individual understanding and connections among those who care about similar topics and questions.

Books, journals, courses, study groups, and online resources—ranging from documentaries to discussion groups—are all valid approaches to gaining knowledge and skills. Because those resources are so abundant and accessible, leaders must approach them with a clear question or a plan. Gone are the days when everyone in a field read the same material at the same time. Similarly, the long waiting periods for requested resources from libraries or bookstores are a thing of the past.

However, ease of access comes at the cost of information overload. A clear question and plan for learning can help leaders organize and prioritize what they wish to learn. Common topics where leaders detect a need to gather new resources include technological applications, self-help, financial matters, and time management techniques. While anyone can benefit from learning about these topics, leaders need to master them, and the necessity for each is intensifying for different reasons.

Most leaders learn new technology because they must. Their community requires them to use an application in order to provide services, leaving them with two choices: dig in their heels and force someone else to do the work, or learn the technology themselves. Few ministers have the human or financial resources to outsource all their technological needs. Whereas self-deprecating comments about being a "luddite" might once have seemed charming, communities now find it difficult to trust ministerial leaders who resist technological innovation. Such resistance wastes time and hinders leaders from reaching the people they are meant to serve. When encountering a new technological necessity, leaders should allocate sufficient time to become familiar with it. Search engines and artificial intelligence can facilitate learning new technologies, but leaders must know how to frame their questions to get the answers they need.

Self-help resources can complement therapy, support groups, theological reflection, and general self-care practices. When a leader encounters obstacles to effective ministry rooted in their conscious or subconscious mind, it is their responsibility to work through those obstacles. The community they serve should not have to accommodate the leader's psychological discomfort. Studying about emotional issues—from codependence to grief to conflict-induced anxiety—can help the leader feel less alone and less helpless than their emotions are telling them they are.

Leaders also have no choice but to think about money, just as they must attend to matters of human resources, strategic planning, and governmental compliance. Much of what non-business leaders know about finance, they learn on the job. That said, financial and managerial concerns often surface early in a leader's career, before they have had the chance to observe the others' trials and gain experience. Therefore, leaders must be prepared to learn about administrative leadership from the start and continue to do so throughout their careers. If serving an institution with an endowment, they must know how the endowment works and what its proceeds can support. If managing a budget, they must understand that budget, no matter what their chief financial officer tells them. Most leaders find that the best way to learn how their budget works is through a combination of studying information and cultivating relationships. Leaders should be determined to understand the budget fully and avoid pretending they comprehend more than they do, as tempting as such pretence might be to protect their ego.

Leaders at one time could master time management without the help of theories, methods, or technologies. For example, a congregational minister could choose to limit the number of evening meetings in which they participated to two per week, block off Monday as a sabbath rest day, and consider themselves ready to manage the stresses of faith-community leadership. Today, various communication portals give communities such broad access to their leaders' time that the leader must devote attention to understanding how they function best and then find resources that maximize and protect their bandwidth. Books, websites, and technological applications that assist in managing time are so broadly available that the leader must, ironically, manage their time as they approach the time management question. Otherwise, their attempts to titrate the demands that come their way will simply feel like a different kind of overwhelming distraction. Those who overconsume time management theories might miss important dimensions of their work out of concern that they are protecting their time.

Creating a Self-Directed Curriculum for Gathering New Content

Factual information is not enough, of course, to save a community, but an open-minded approach to what the culture requires of its citizens can be a first step toward widespread transformation. Key to cultivating open-mindedness are beliefs that curiosity is healthy and that learning is important. Institutions of all kinds face questions about their relevance in the twenty-first century that would have been inconceivable to their twentieth-century counterparts. Much of what fosters leadership development involves not actions, but attitudes. Leaders who approach their profession with curiosity—as learners rather than as experts who feel they should already know everything—naturally engage with cultural change as they navigate the world. This inclination to ask questions and learn from interactions with people, communities, and trends generates openness and responsiveness in those around them. An ongoing desire for lifelong learning helps both leaders and their constituents remain hopeful about the human condition and humanity's place in the world.

Leaders must budget their time and attention when developing themselves and pace themselves to be able to continue to function rather than ingesting huge amounts of content that they cannot absorb or apply. The voracious reader, listener to podcasts, and viewer of documentaries might accumulate a great deal of information, but if the only way they use it is to quote it back to (bored) people in conversations, the data overload has not contributed to genuine growth. Data transmission is one of the easiest forms of professional development to access, but the quantity of content taken in does not define the quality of the leaders' new knowledge, skills, or habits. The challenge lies in gathering the right amount and type of information, while conserving enough energy for more demanding practices such as integrating new knowledge and being open not just to new information but also to new ways of thinking. Leaders must have enough energy after absorbing new ideas to reflect upon them and commit to putting them into action.

Graduate-level education for leadership provides the leader with content and strategies to address their curiosity. When they write papers, for example, students in professional education settings must frame a question, seek the resources to answer it, and use those resources to create new ideas and new knowledge. Repeating the process of asking and answering questions helps students develop the habit of approaching uncertainty by forming questions, seeking out resources, integrating those resources, and drawing conclusions with practical implications for their field.

However, graduate students are not the only ones capable of strategic inquiry. They are simply more accustomed to thinking through questions thoroughly and often. Formal higher education teaches people how to learn, but others can develop skills for research and analysis in other ways. The mentality needed to create a self-guided curriculum for professional development starts with curiosity. But curiosity alone is not enough; framing good questions and sampling sources strategically are crucial skills for navigating the overwhelming amount of available information.

Dissertation writers and AI prompt engineers alike understand that getting a well-formulated question is essential to arriving at a good answer. Many leaders, however, make the mistake by rushing past the task of posing and clarifying questions and dive headfirst into activity. They form task forces to address an issue without articulating a specific question for that task force to tackle. They hire people, devote resources, and make promises, yet absent a clear question, everyone involved finds themselves working toward different ends. Pausing to frame a question must is one of the leader's most important responsibilities. While it may not take long, the costs of skipping this step can be high.

Many leaders and their followers mistakenly think that bold, prophetic leadership must be impulsive and spontaneous. They ask, "Why not just act since it's the right thing to do?" Leaders can and do choose their actions based on what is right, even when facing unpopularity or criticism. They must, however, first articulate the problem they are trying to solve. Similarly, leaders often rush into learning without clearly identifying where they must grow in effectiveness.

Just as leaders must act deliberately and strategically when managing others, they must frame a good question before engaging in learning so that they do not waste energy on solving the wrong problem. For example, a manager who finds that employees keep quitting may benefit from a course on supervising staff but needs to determine whether they are doing something to contribute to their employees' decisions. A leader can act swiftly and still proceed carefully; the two are not mutually exclusive. The leader who leaps before looking is not brave but rather afraid to stop and think—exactly when stopping and thinking is what their community needs most.

Once the question is framed, the leader can break it down into component parts in order to determine the next steps for strategic information gathering. They then decide who or what can best answer their questions through a process called "sampling." Researchers use sampling strategies when preparing for sociological or market research. Once they have a question defined, they ask where the relevant data can be found: "Who can answer this question, and how can we gain access to those people or sources most efficiently?" Strategic sampling, whether from written sources or people, is, just like framing good prompts, more important now than ever. Data sources include literature as well as insights from people who have provide valuable answers to the leader's question.

Data sources in the form of literature can take the form of published information or unpublished written documents. When a new leader assumes a role, they are usually advised to go through old files—meeting minutes, newsletters, rosters, budgets, and other documents that tell the story of the institution they are entering. Additionally, they should familiarize themselves with published materials that describe and analyze the wider field. This wider sweep transcends any one institution and sheds light on the needs affecting all institutions. However, the sheer volume of written documents can overwhelm the one seeking answers, making it essential to approach such resources with a careful strategy and clearly framed questions.

As recently as the 1980s and 1990s, doctoral candidates were expected to consult and cite every single resource relevant to their topic. Today, citing everything on a subject is in many cases impossible, due to the sheer number of available resources, including many that are unreliable. Depending on the field, expectations for originality have shifted as well. For example, while an archaeologist cannot present a new finding that has also already been claimed by another, a social scientist might generate something new by placing ideas from two different disciplines in dialogue with one another.[4]

Comprehensiveness is no longer the standard by which seekers of expertise measure success. Instead, they strategize on how to find the most relevant information as efficiently as possible—prioritizing quality over quantity, relevance over volume. Learners have many options: reading theoretical texts or marketing materials, talking to people to gather wisdom, and listening to groups of people to gain general impressions. These practices—foraging for knowledge and reading, talking and listening to people—might seem obvious. Yet few leaders approach this work methodically and intentionally, and as a result, when they become busy and overwhelmed, these practices often fall by the wayside. When this happens, leaders close themselves off to learning that could make their work more effective at the very moment that new insights could help them the most.

Leaders can overcome such distractions and lack of focus by treating their information-gathering efforts as methodical tasks, similar to other items on their to-do lists. One way they might build a methodology for gathering content is what was described previously as "strategic sampling." When statisticians confront a question where they cannot connect with every individual who might have knowledge to share in a study, they sample. When an advertisement for toothpaste claims, "Four out of five dentists surveyed said…," it is clear that the market researchers did not speak with every dentist on earth. They spoke with a sample, and they deemed that sample to be representative. Learners who wish to get their questions answered but are overwhelmed by the volume of information available to them can do the same thing without raising questions about their research ethics. Human beings must sample selectively because their time, attention, and capacity to integrate data are all limited. Artificial intelligence might not suffer such limitations, but it also cannot make ethical decisions—at least not yet—about approaching human research participants as those who could be adversely affected by research questions. Of course, AI's capacity is changing by the minute.

One exercise that can aid in strategic sampling is to imagine a brick wall.

When a leader takes apart their leadership development question into component parts, they can see the gap in their knowledge from a different point of view. That leader might have information about many bricks in the wall, but they must organize their learning around information gaps. This following fictional scenario illustrates the kinds of situations where a leader might benefit from content-based leadership learning:

Sandrine leads a faith community that wants to connect more meaningfully with its neighborhood. Her church is a short walk from the local junior high school and shares a plot of land with the town's public library, which has strict policies about unaccompanied children coming to the library after school. Sandrine is aware

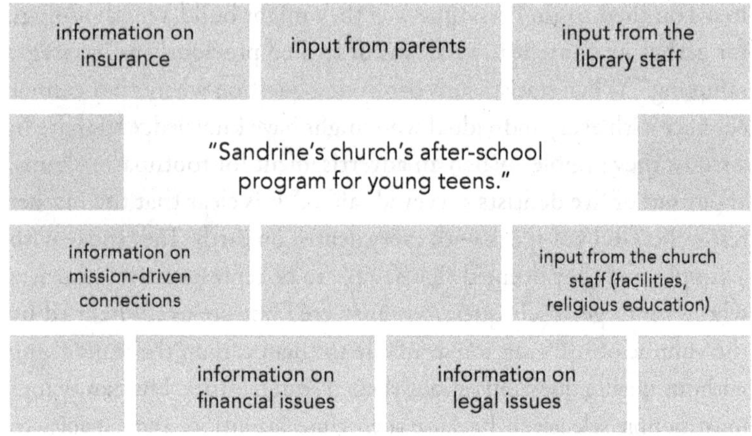

Figure 4.1.

that many parents of preteens and young teens in the community don't have options for after-school programming. Unable to leave work to drive their kids to sports or clubs, parents must choose between having their children take the bus home or letting them loiter around the school until they arrive. Kids would prefer to be together, of course, but the public library cannot handle the influx of young patrons without adult supervision.

Sandrine and the leaders in her church wonder what it would take to start a middle-school after-school program where students could participate in supervised outings, crafts, games, and sports. The community has a clear need, the church has the facility and proximity, but no one knows where to begin. Sandrine can help the community's leaders by breaking their questions down into more manageable pieces so they might explore various possibilities (figure 4.1).

Options for data collection include surveys, interviews, and focus groups. Sandrine and others should gather these data to make sure that they fully understand the community's needs and nuances. Next, Sandrine should direct information-gathering efforts on the population to be served, recognizing that younger teens have specific developmental needs. Sandrine can take the lead in gathering literature and advice methodically about what the church would need to offer the community to add value to what is already available. Led by Sandrine, they can gather information about the legal and financial dimensions of creating a new program, which would both serve the community but also expose the church to expenses and risks.

With full information available, Sandrine can compile findings and offer recommendations, connecting those recommendations with the mission of the church. So often, however, leaders do not even begin the exploration process, because the task of gathering knowledge feels insurmountable. The brick-wall exercise helps counteract feelings of overwhelm that can hinder creative inquiry.

Leaders require a method for approaching the unknown, or it will overwhelm them. Conventional wisdom suggests that leaders should bring about change slowly, only after fully understanding the context and the repercussions of change. Realistically, however, leaders are rarely "ready" to make changes when their constituents demand them. Therefore, they must attend to the reasoning behind the conventional wisdom: Leaders should bring about change only after learning its possible ramifications, and learning takes time. But nor can content-based learning be comprehensive today, so a sampling strategy and brick-wall exercise are essential to moving forward.

Overwhelm is but one of the barriers leaders face when they need professional development that involves gathering and integrating new information. They must also overcome their all-too-human insecurity about gaps in their knowledge, what with the feelings of ego-hurt and impostor syndrome that accompany this insecurity. They must learn to live with the fact that constituents in their care look to them for answers and do not respond well when their leader cannot provide them on demand. A methodical approach to gathering and staying current on field-related information can help manage both ego and expectations. With a plan for how they will continue to grow in knowledge, the leader will be able to approach the unknown and respond to questions with greater confidence, keeping anxiety down to manageable levels and making the implementation of this methodology for getting questions answered more realistic.

Benefits of Graduate Theological Education for Content-Based Learning

Not all communal leaders have attended graduate school in their profession. The advantages of such attendance are not obvious and are not necessarily what those in the leader's care might expect. Graduate theological education for ministry is not primarily beneficial to students and eventual professionals because of the information provided in their classes and books. Rather, the greatest benefit lies in learning how to learn. For instance, a seminary student might take one or two courses on the New Testament, where they analyze various books and passages from the perspective of the text's historical context and current relevance. They then use these exegetical skills to make sense of other texts in the Old and New Testaments, and even for interpreting other types of literature.

Factual recall is not what makes graduate theological education foundational. Instead, graduate school students learn how to frame questions and find answers. Although graduates might not have obscure information at their fingertips, they need not look far to find it. Graduate school in the professions helps learners feel confident in the face of the utterly unfamiliar. It can transform the learner's sense of curiosity from of anxiety to excitement. Graduate theological education also offers the learner the companionship of colleagues who normalize the reality that no one knows everything. Being surrounded by others whose intellects they respect, and who also have questions and gaps in their knowledge, helps transform impostor syndrome into a shared sense of discovery.

Whether or not a person has attended graduate school, they still require methods for meeting their content-based information needs throughout their professional years. Graduate school can offer these methods, but whether the student adopts them or not depends on the individual and their learning experience. Those inside or outside of graduate school can gather and read books, delve into courses, seek out information from constituents in a methodical way, solicit advice from mentors, and engage in informational consultations with colleagues. In addition to a base layer of content and information, graduate school provides practices that shape the curious person into a dedicated seeker and pursuer of knowledge.

Professional Skills and Responsibility for Imparting Them

Graduate theological educators and other purveyors of learning for professions are often unsure about their roles in teaching students the necessary skills for their fields. Seminary faculty tend to educate on abstract topics. The responsibility for moving students from the abstract to the concrete remains a matter of ongoing debate. Some suggest that students will learn to bring their intellectual attainments down to earth through internships. Others argue that this happens on the job, after graduation. Still others believe that the greatest challenges seminary graduates will face are ones not yet known, making education focused on skills too short-lived to justify its emphasis. Ultimately, graduates need enough skill to handle their responsibilities upon graduation so they can navigate their early days of service without becoming liabilities to the institutions they are called to serve—and someday transform.

In his seminal work on education for professional competence, Donald Schön argues that skills and knowledge cannot be separated.[5] In *Educating the Reflective Practitioner*, Schön disputes the notion that educators should teach for deep knowledge and then have students "apply" that knowledge through skill later. He contends that the work of learning for leadership begins with skill, or what he calls "artistry." According to Schön, the practitioner must first consider what is required of the leader by way of skill and then work backward to determine which theory should be taught and learned.[6] He categorizes skill learning into three "arts": problem framing, implementation, and improvisation. All three arts are areas where a novice can begin immediately and where a professional can continue to grow over years or even decades.

Schön and his colleague, Chris Argyris, critique the academy's divisions subject matter into "theory" and "practice," asserting that such binaries may define the academy and faculty but are ultimately inaccurate for professionals.[7] They object to the notion that skills and ideas should be separated when educating practitioners, as all learning requires elements of both, particularly when a learner is entering a field characterized by change and a need to grow in capacity to address the unknown. This inaccurate and unhelpful separation between learning skills and learning ideas often banishes skills from the classroom under the assumption that they are being learned elsewhere.[8]

Levels of learning that span outward from lived experience to abstract thinking have their place, argued Schön. He presented three layers of learning that could guide learning for leadership education when describing "the practicum," or the educational setting where skills, knowledge, and wisdom for the future intermingle from the outset. The practicum integrates different forms of knowledge and understandings of what knowledge and epistemologies. When carried out effectively, the practicum can teach skills, form identity, and prepare the professional for the unforeseeable. If a person believes that professional learning requires internalizing facts and procedures, the practicum can function as technical training. If they believe professional learning relates more to identity formation, what Schön describes as "thinking like a [insert profession],"then the practicum provides "reflection-in-action through which practitioners sometimes make sense of uncertain, unique or conflicted situations of practice."[9]

Despite their own research on educating architects, Argyris and Schön point to religious leadership as the originator of modern professions. Priests were the original professionals, as they were granted superhuman authority within the church, which extended to the community beyond the religious sanctuary. Over time, they write, professionals became differentiated and secularized, but the vesting of *authority* within a *setting* became the model that guided the emergence of secular professions. As professions broadened, the importance of a blessing from a supernatural being diminished, while technical mastery grew in significance. The expertise assigned to professions became the basis for elevating professionals above other workers, leading to the idea that a professional is granted sacred autonomy within their context because of their technical expertise.[10]

A blessing from God and technical mastery are vastly different sources of authority. Theological educators resist the notion that they are primarily responsible for teaching techniques or skills, and this resistance is understandable, as skills-based knowledge can only take the aspiring professional so far. To be prepared to serve and face an unknown future, the seminary student must also be prepared to think like a minister and engage in reflective practice throughout their lifetime.

Neglecting of skills-based learning shortchanges the learner in two ways. First, such neglect fails to provide the learner with a launching point from which they might pursue lifelong learning for greater competence and creativity. Second, neglecting to teach students skills overlooks what the wider culture understands a professional to know, be, and do. Educators set their graduates up for disappointment when constituents discover that—even with a diploma in hand—their leader does not possess basic skills. Those deeply reflective but as yet unskilled graduates are likely to respond to constituents' disappointment not by reaching out to gather the skills-based information they need, but through defensive withdrawal.

Pretending they are above the wider culture's fascination with technical skill and competence, insisting that depth is more important, could needlessly lower the minister's status in the wider culture. Eschewing technical expertise does not make a leader seem "deep" but rather out of touch with societal expectations of their craft. Furthermore, aloofness in the face of a need for skills-based learning cuts the leader off from the most challenging, interesting, and formative questions of the times. The emergence of new skills accompanies the emergence of new ways of thinking.

The Ethics of Learning Content, Information, and Skills in the Early- to Mid-Twenty-First Century

In a profession as metaphysical, mystical, and complex as ministry, it is difficult to imagine a task that could be designated a skill and nothing more. When ministers had to learn to use technology to connect communities during the COVID-19 pandemic, for example, they had to go beyond figuring out how the technology worked. They needed to consider how to make people feel welcome in online settings, how to ensure that worship was conducted reverently using applications not previously used for that purpose, and what theology and doctrine would guide practice. Technological skills were part of the discernment process, but connected to them were loftier questions where communities relied on their ministers for guidance. Knowing how to use technology was just the beginning.

Learning skills and content might be considered the most concrete, and therefore least ethically challenging, forms of lifelong learning for leadership. Beyond technical questions of competence, the matters with which leaders concern themselves become immediately more complicated. For example, ministerial leaders need information, instruction, and skills-based knowledge to function ethically. If their compensation comes from donated money, they must steward the time they devote to ministry so that they can honestly tell their donors that they have used resources in a way that honors the donors' intentions. To even understand the nature of "donor intent" as a legal construct, the leader needs knowledge of how nonprofits function. The leader who is paid with donated money might intuitively realize the ethical demand that they work hard for reasons beyond their callings from God and their inner drive, but knowledge about how funds and philanthropy bind them to the state as well as the church helps them to think clearly about the ethics of time stewardship.

Another example is the need for ministerial leaders to do more than rely on good instincts when it comes to maintaining professional boundaries. Boundary management is as much a skill- and content-based area of study as it is an attitude. Those newer to ministerial leadership benefit greatly from basic training in boundary awareness: Do not engage in intimate relations with those who understand you to be their minister; do not accept pricey gifts from those to whom you might need to tell a hard truth; do take excellent care of yourself so you remember who you are. Over time, boundary awareness deepens into a place of ongoing reflective practice, but that too requires disciplined attention through professional education throughout the minister's career.

Newer questions related to the ethics of skill- and information-based learning for ministry arise from changes in the institutional church. The institutional church is undergoing sweeping, seismic change. The structures that hold it up are, in some cases, under scrutiny to the point where their futures are uncertain. Content-based learning for ministry that enables those institutional structures to continue—propping them up despite the forces of gravity pulling them down—might be considered harmful in a collusive way. Some might argue that it would be better for ministers to allow the institutional structures that undergird faith communities to collapse so that something new can emerge.

The argument that ministers should not learn how to service faltering institutions makes no sense in a liminal season. The principles of emergent leadership do not suggest that incompetent leaders are best suited to bring about change. Rather, theories of emergence indicate that a leader in an in-between era must be able to sustain communities as they are, allowing God to draw out of them the new thing they need to become. Leaders who do not possess and cannot learn skills are not poised to bring about the change faith communities need to move into a post-institutional future. Instead, their incompetence will harm institutions and individuals desperate for a leader they can trust to hold things together until a new way is made known.

A second contemporary challenge to information, skills, and knowledge learning for professional effectiveness in ministry is the arrival of artificial intelligence. Even before AI could write sermons and conduct constituent-based research, it was relieving brains of the necessity of remembering facts. AI will prove itself extremely helpful for skills-based learning, as it simplifies the process of curating resources. The ministerial leader can command it to suggest the best books, articles, websites, scholars, and courses to help them get their questions answered. But the ministerial leader's knowledge of how to frame questions so that AI can understand them, and their discernment as to what they do not know and need to learn, has never been more important.

AI cannot tell the ministerial leader their greatest liabilities. It cannot elucidate where they need to strengthen their knowledge of the latest practices and methods, although it can help them do so once a question is framed. A photographic memory might have been the gold standard for knowledge in a pre-AI era, but today the ultimate in content knowledge is insight into the right questions a leader needs to ask for the sake of the community, so that leaders focus on the important—not just the urgent or what constituents pressure them to prioritize.

The capacity to frame and pose questions might become more challenging, generation by generation, if a time comes when young professionals have never had to memorize anything. It is not yet known whether rote memorization, deliberate, slow problem-solving, and the necessity of addressing problems without billions of answers at one's fingertips was important preparation for using AI effectively today.[11] AI will make the leadership learner who wants to access content, information, and training for skills far more successful and require them to waste far less time finding what they need. Whether their minds will be prepared to internalize new knowledge and integrate it into practice is less certain.

AI might throw off the balance of different forms of lifelong learning for leadership, which must include more than simply gathering information. Because content-based learning and locating information are now easier than ever, leaders might default to gathering facts as their go-to method of self-development. This is natural for a busy person with heavy responsibilities, as it follows the path of least resistance. However, new knowledge about the way the human brain functions challenges the leadership learner to rise above fact-based, content-oriented learning, so as to stretch the mind and focus on the big, strategic picture.

In his book *The Wise Advocate: The Inner Voice of Strategic Leadership*,[12] Art Kleiner writes that leaders must train their brains to focus on higher priorities regularly—daily and hourly—if they want to be strategic change-makers. If not trained otherwise, minds naturally sink into the weeds of details and problem-solving, writes Kleiner, at the expense of the big picture and what is important. In teaching change leadership, Kleiner begins class sessions with mindfulness meditation to demonstrate the value of regularly instructing the brain on where to focus. His students discover that directing their attention in their preferred direction becomes easier through mindfulness practice. So does concentrating on strategic priorities rather than complicated, but ultimately unimportant, problems.

Leadership Education Through Content
Whose Responsibility?

To describe a leader as someone who "knows their stuff" is high praise. That said, no leader is born knowing all they need to know, and expectations for what one must know change quickly. Gone are the days of leaders coming into their roles with all the answers. Today's leader needs to know how to frame questions and get them answered—quickly and competently. Leaders must face the expectation that they should already possess all the information one could possibly need to be deemed trustworthy. Constituents must be trained to feel more confidence in leaders who tell them how they will figure out what is not yet known and who have the necessary skills to gain such competence.

Leaders need information, skills, and knowledge to carry out their responsibilities. They must know their fields, the culture and its evolution, the happenings in peer institutions, their constituents, and the practices that make up their professions. Whose responsibility is it to ensure that they attain content-based knowledge? In some fields, licensing boards require continuing education, and such is the case for ministers with ordained standing in some faith traditions. Given the sheer amount of change surrounding professions and professionals, however, no external driver will suffice to propel the leader to stay current. Information is too abundant, and making decisions about what, and how much, information to gather is a constant challenge.

Graduate schools, including graduate theological schools that prepare ministers, demonstrate uncertainty about their roles in conveying skills. Information about scripture, and abstract information about theology and ethics, maintain a place of privilege in the curriculum, while instruction in skills often falls to practitioners without a theoretical basis undergirding their knowledge. The tacit message from a curriculum that places the abstract above the practical is clear: Anyone can learn and carry out a skill, and the true intellectual should place their attention on loftier things.

Based on what is now known about the brain, this hierarchy is not necessarily wrong, but it is right for reasons that might surprise members of Bible and theology faculty departments. Attuning one's attention to the bigger picture, rather than becoming lost in the weeds of content, is harder to do than it is to gather facts and learn skills. The leader must discipline their mind to rise above the fray, making attention a crucial mental exercise for training the leader's mind beyond the immediate and the details.

Conclusion

The ideal approach to learning information, knowledge, and skills is to gather enough of them before embarking on a profession to protect the community from the harm the ill-informed leader might cause. Then, the leader ought to balance content-based leadership learning with other forms of leadership development, framing questions narrowly enough to avoid falling down rabbit holes of information, conserving time and energy for reflective practice and horizon expansion.

CHAPTER FIVE

Leadership Development Through Fostering Theological Reflection

"WHAT IS THE difference between twenty-five years of ministerial leadership experience and one year of ministerial leadership experience, twenty-five times? Reflective practice." This aphorism, phrased as a joke, captures the importance of reflection to the practice of leadership, especially ministerial leadership. Those who learn from their experiences improve in their competence. Those who intentionally engage in theological reflection inspired by experience, asking questions about God's will in human activities, become stronger in their faith.

The urgent need for deep reflective practice for leadership development at this moment, even more pressingly than in past eras, is no joke. In an era of careening cultural change, the most important and interesting ministerial leadership challenges are ones no one has experienced before. No training manual exists for such situations, but lived experience can function as the minister's textbook. The expression, "Make every day a school day" grows out of the assumption that leaders are reflecting on their new experiences in a methodical, intentional way. Leaders' constituents sometimes scapegoat their leaders for not knowing what could not have been known, and those leaders become discouraged and burned out, rather than curious and engaged. Therefore, leaders must dedicate themselves to reflective practice, even in the face of indications from the wider world that doing so is less valuable than it most certainly is.

Although content-based, skills-oriented programs for lifelong learning in leadership beyond graduate professional schools are easy to find and access, they might not always offer the most effective lifelong learning. Many scholars of adult education consider reflective practice to be the gold standard for leadership growth over time. Reflection grounds the leader in learning, training them to respond rather than react. If they can regard all the challenges they face as opportunities to grow, rather than burdens, they approach even their most stubborn and intractable problems the way a climber approaches a mountain. That said, finding outlets and opportunities for reflective practice requires effort, intentionality, attention, and time.

Traditional, Classical Reflective Practices for Leadership Development

Those seeking to learn leadership are well served by placing themselves in settings where cross-grained experiences are extremely likely to happen, and where supports are in place to both gather those experiences and transform them into knowledge and wisdom. Supervised experience is a venerable teacher. "Experience" suggests that the learner immerses themselves in a situation ripe for challenge. "Supervised" suggests the presence of a safety net. That net could include guidance, risk management that resists and refrains from placing recipients of ministry in spiritual harm's way, and opportunities for the leadership learner to intentionally derive meaning from challenges. Supervised experience sends the learner into unfamiliar, provocative, and evocative opportunities to serve. It is part simulation, too, in that, when designed well, a supervised experience can only go so wrong.

Theological Reflection

Graduate theological schools introduced theological reflection as a mode of ministry-learning in the mid-twentieth century alongside the advent of credit-earning supervised ministry. Seminary students began during those years to engage in internships not just to supplement their income, but as part of their curriculum. Theological reflection was the educational modality that transformed fieldwork into field education.

Typically, today and in recent generations, students serving in internship settings meet weekly with a minister trained in supervision for the purpose of theological reflection. They might submit a written reflection ahead of time that captures a thought or incident from the ministry setting. Then, during a supervision session, the student and the supervisor delve into the reflection and make sense of it through the lenses of faith.

Education for professional competence through theological reflection can prepare and deepen the practice of both beginners and seasoned practitioners alike. For beginners, theological reflection models invert what one might consider the expected sequence. Conventionally, a student pursuing a profession might expect someone to provide them with knowledge and skills about how to carry out a task, and that this provision would be comprehensive and over an extended period of time. Then, the beginner implements the learning and receives feedback after the fact. In an approach to preparing ministers that relies on theological reflection, or an action–reflection sequence for professionals in any field, the beginner receives only the lightest instruction and is thrown into the work of ministry as one throws a learner into a pool to swim. Then, the learner devotes more time to theological reflection through writing and discussion with a supervisor.

The latter sequence—light instruction, action, deep reflection—takes seriously the way adult minds learn new information. Adults come to learning with minds already formed. Their new experiences must connect with their preconceptions and past learnings, or the adult will simply forget what they hear. The educator must foster connections between experience and theory for the learner. Therefore, starting instruction with a recent lived experience is more likely to cause the adult learner to internalize new facts and information. Reflecting on new learnings anchors them in the practitioner's psyche. Therefore, teaching a minister to carry out a new skill does not necessitate emphasizing the transmission of information. An action–reflection model, or a learning approach that includes experience followed by theological reflection, can be helpful to the learner in their earliest days of practice.

Theological reflection is also a practice that a person can carry out over the course of a ministry career. One of the great benefits of a life in ministry is that each day presents new challenges based on the changing nature of the context in which ministry takes place. To harness the benefits of ministry's constant surprises, rather than resenting their inconveniences, the leader is well served by an attitude of curiosity about what God is trying to tell the minister through the experiences God is sending their way.

Among the many benefits of theological reflection as a form of leadership development, its contemporaneity ensures that learners stay on the cutting edge. Those who engage in theological reflection in real time need not worry about their skills becoming obsolete. They will face situations not yet encountered or anticipated with the skills needed to learn and adapt in real time.

Another advantage of theological reflection is the mentoring and collegial accountability built into its practice. A person can reflect theologically on their own, of course, but the practice is built for reasoning together. Because the ministerial leader is bound to encounter those who are different from themselves, allowing others into their reflections on the meaning of patterns and events they observe in their ministries is key to their learning and accountability. Since no one ministers alone, it is difficult to imagine the ministerial leadership autodidact.

Theological reflection provides grist for conversation between supervisors and supervisees, the writer and their audience, and among colleagues. Leaders serve communities with deeply ingrained historical patterns and emotional systems resistant to change. Those trained in theological reflection default to bringing partners into the questions, including confidants both outside the ministry context and within it. The habit of sharing their biggest and most puzzling questions about God's action in a community improves ministers' relationships and models an attitude of curiosity over consternation.

The leadership development practice of theological reflection, as the Sunday School song goes, "builds its house upon the rock." Leaders who, with all deliberate intentionality, rely on God to make sense of the world develop a sense of groundedness that transcends even the most supportive collegial or mentoring relationships. By shining the light of faith on experience, theological reflection can resurrect possibilities for new life from what seemed like death-dealing blows to a leader's confidence or a community's viability. As the psalmist writes, "God is in the midst of her; she shall not be moved" (Psalm 45:6a).

The Ministry of Supervision

In a one-on-one dialogue with a trained supervisor, the learner and supervisor together consider the contents of a critical incident report. They hold the incident described up to the light of faith and make initial observations about the theological implications of events. Learner and supervisor together ask questions like, "Where was God in the midst of that moment?" "What scriptures does the event bring to mind?" "What does the world require of ministers at moments like those? How can they be of greatest help to others?" In some cases, learners send their written reflections to supervisors ahead of time, and the supervisor writes back or comes prepared. The key to the effectiveness of theological reflection under supervision has less to do with sequence and more to do with the intentionality required to set aside time to think, write, and converse about the meaning of ministry work. Rather than clocking experiences and setting them aside, theological reflection turns them into lessons that improve ministers' effectiveness on three levels: professional effectiveness, personal faith, and spiritual leadership.

Training for ministry supervisors, whether they are the learner's pastor or employer, must include recognizing that they and the one under their supervision are not the same person. One of the most helpful things a supervisor can do when a learner presents a critical incident report is to help the learner bracket their own assumptions about who was right and who was wrong or what "should" have happened. They cannot help another find objectivity if they do not possess it themselves. Many seminaries offer and require training for those working with student ministers, even when supervisors have vast ministry experience, as the ministry of supervision includes many nuances that are not obvious.

Although it sometimes surprises students and supervisors alike, the ministry of supervision has less to do with teaching tasks and more to do with reflecting with the learner after a task has been carried out. Emphasizing reflection over skills might not seem natural to a minister supervising a learner to carry out duties with which they are deeply familiar. Yet, learning through reflective practice gives budding ministers a chance to make those duties their own in a way that deepens their practice from the beginning. Reflection, as opposed to task-coaching, is a different kind of teaching tool than most professionals are ready to use. Therefore, training helps them bracket their own competence in favor of fostering that of those under their supervision.

In the supervisory consultation, the learner and the supervisor dissect the selected incident and ask deeper questions about it. Provocative supervisory questions might include, "What were you most afraid would happen?" and "What do you think God was trying to show you?" In conversation, the learner begins to close the gap between what they think they believe and how they actually live their lives and carry out their ministries. Some educators call this an identification of the distance between a person's espoused theology and their operational theology. Becoming aware of—and reducing—this distance is a valid goal for supervision.

Finding such gaps should not be understood as uncovering the learner's hypocrisy, for no one knows what actions they might take under pressure until presented with the need to take action. Paul the Apostle, and even Jesus himself, discovered gaps between what they *said* they wanted to do and what they actually did—what they did and what they knew ought to be done. Under supervision, the learner cultivates habits of telling the truth and grounding their actions in their beliefs about God. Through repeated practice, they grow more comfortable with examining even their most embarrassing, frightening, or shameful choices, knowing that something new and good might emerge from them.

Adequately processing the event requires partnership and accountability. In *From Ministry to Theology: Pastoral Action and Reflection*, John Patton writes, "Adequate theological reflection on pastoral practice requires immersion in the clinical material of human experience, inhibition of hasty interpretation and conceptualization of it, and consultation about it with colleagues involved in a similar ministry."[1] When challenged, leaders are bound to react with feelings before formulating thoughts. Their feelings are instructive but should not be considered authoritative. An attitude of curiosity, and willingness to submit to another person's interpretation with knowledge of the context, helps the leader sort through their feelings and find, underneath them, nuggets of wisdom. Supervisors help the learner stay with uncomfortable feelings long enough for wisdom to emerge from the fog of emotions.

The term "supervisor" should not be conflated with "boss" in the ministry of supervised reflective practice. The learner can empower a boss, peer, or colleague to help them investigate critical incidents and where God was in the midst of them. Whether in pairs, supervisor/supervisee mentoring sessions, small groups, staff teams, or other forms of intentional gathering, theological reflection can happen in many formats. The supervisee subordinates themselves to the supervisor not solely because of that person's job title but because they are willing to allow the supervisor to shine light on what they might otherwise avoid seeing.

The term "supervisor" in the context of reflective practice describes roles in a relationship at a particular point in time. "Supervision" is a correct, if problematic, term for describing the person who guides theological reflection. Usually, supervisors are bosses who care more about the organization's missional success or productivity than about the employee. In the context of leadership development, the supervisor supports the learning of another in their care. The learner surrenders the responsibility of guiding meaning-making to another so they can focus on their own growth. This use of "supervisor" and "supervision" becomes important in describing the leadership development practice of supervised experience. Under the guidance of a supervisor, a ministry learner can transform failures, surprises (good and bad), and inspirations into materials with which they build their character, discover their personal styles, and construct their ministerial identities.

Current Practices in Graduate Theological Education

In graduate theological education, two approaches to action–reflection models for learning dominate the landscape: supervised ministry and Clinical Pastoral Education (CPE). Seminaries offer supervised ministry programs, also known as Theological Field Education, where students engage in internships under the supervision of a minister trained by the seminary. Students serve a set number of hours per week, carrying out ministry duties directly connected to their learning goals. They engage in theological reflection with their supervisors and often work with a group of peers in practicum-style learning, comparing notes with other supervised-ministry students, all under the guidance of a member of the seminary's instructional staff or faculty.

CPE differs from supervised ministry in specific ways that are not always obvious to the layperson. First, seminaries do not offer CPE. Sites that offer CPE are accredited by an agency—increasingly multiple agencies—that monitor the sites for quality, ethics, and truth-in-advertising. Students may register through their seminaries to earn credit for CPE via cross-registration or transfer of credits, which often confusing learners into thinking that the two forms of experience-based learning—supervised ministry and CPE—are interchangeable. Although the two methods may appear similar in students' lived experiences, supervised ministry is part of a degree program's overall goals, while CPE operates independently of those goals. CPE settings emphasize the role of ministers as chaplains to individuals, whereas supervised ministry encompasses a wider range of roles, with the goal of training ministry generalists.

Because readiness to minister amid crisis is important, some faith traditions insist on ordaining only candidates for ministry with one unit (300-400 hours of supervised chaplaincy) of CPE. They also expect one year of supervised ministry in a setting connected with the tradition's denomination. These conventions are shifting and changing with time, but general expectations for ministers' preparation have rested stable for three generations: supervision of the learner in high-stress chaplaincy roles, combined with mentoring in community-leading generalists roles, forms the basic action–reflection learning for aspiring ministers.

Both CPE and supervised ministry take place in ministry settings, giving learners opportunities practice under the guidance of trained professionals. The best settings allow students to try everything the most senior minister does, offering access the widest possible range of ministry tasks. In less ideal settings, students may be relegated to observer roles without meaningful duties. Educators help students find settings that challenge them to stretch and take risks, followed by deep reflection, which fosters growth in competence and character alike.

In CPE, learners—typically seminary students—minister to people undergoing some of the hardest moments they will ever face. They work with those suffering involuntary hardships, such as patients, incarcerated persons, or residents in care facilities. Thus, learners intentionally place themselves in challenging situations alongside those in their care. CPE settings include hospitals, prisons, rehabilitation centers, and institutions dedicated to serving the unhoused. While hospitals remain the primary CPE setting, new forms of CPE are emerging, including online programs where students find their own clinical sites and receive online supervision.

Participants in CPE programs provide people in ministry settings with support and care, and then reflect with a supervisor and group on what they did and learned. CPE's methodology incorporates theological reflection alongside practices borrowed from social work and psychology, such as "verbatims." In a verbatim, learners write word-for-word accounts of their encounters with clients and share these with peers for feedback to improve their pastoral care practices. By blending theological learning with social science techniques, CPE offers students a multidisciplinary framework for experiencing ministry, gaining new insights, and developing new skills.

Theological reflection takes place on various levels in both CPE and supervised ministry. Most learners in such programs are expected to write weekly "critical incident reports," which capture actual incidents or surprising insights. These reports include detailed descriptions of events, the choices made, the emotions felt, and some preliminary reflections on their meaning. However, supervision is where the deepest reflection happens.

CPE and supervised ministry employ other reflective practice methods, beyond one-on-one supervision with a textual critical incident report at its center and theological reflection as the common denominator. CPE students meet in groups to share encounters, receive feedback, and discuss choices made and alternatives considered. Some CPE programs require learners to seek out feedback from those who have received their ministry or borne witness to it. These intentional reflective practices deepen, and even broaden, learning. They can also be more emotionally challenging. For instance, visiting a sick patient in a hospital might bring some insights and cause some overwhelm, but receiving peer critique on the visit is outside the norm of ordinary learning and can offer new, sometimes unsettling, self-awareness.

The critical incident report begins with the ministry learner selecting an event—typically one that is surprising or disruptive and continues to occupy their thoughts. Theological educator Kenneth Pohly refers to such moments, , whether they involve conflict or disappointment, as "rough places."[2] Critical incident reports help smooth these rough edges, transforming difficult memories from sources of shame and self-blame into lessons that foster growth. Transformation, however, is not automatic. The learner must shine the light of experience, faith, prior knowledge, and the accumulated wisdom of the Christian tradition onto these "rough places." This process is most effective under supervision.

Professional learning through reflective practice disrupts the assumed sequence of achieving competence. Instead of receiving instruction, practicing, and then receiving feedback, the process begins with an attempt at a professional skill, followed by mentored reflection, which leads to new insights. The learner then reinvests these insights in future practice, completing a learning loop.

This learning loop, characteristic of formal graduate theological education in both supervised ministries and CPE, breaks down quickly after the ministerial leader enters professional practice. Mentored "residencies" after graduation are few and far between. Some first ministry positions include team participation, while others do not. Without a team, ministers must find theological reflection partners, a challenge in a culture of time scarcity where ministers are expected to operate at the limits of their capacity. Time scarcity is not conducive to reflection, so ministers must squeeze it in where they can.

In an attempt to fit reflection into their schedules, some ministers turn reflective opportunities into obligations, such as sermon preparation or pastoral care. Seeking reflection through ministering to those in the minister's care involves a role reversal—risking boundary violations. Quickly after graduating, ministry learners must develop a self-guided plan for ongoing reflective practice. Seminary educators do well to inculcate habits of reflective practice, modeling collegial support and reinforcing the value of mentors.

Emerging Practices in Graduate Theological Education

Graduate theological education has changed rapidly in the twenty-first century due to numerous, intersecting factors. The end of Christendom at the close of the modern era gave way to the proliferation of different religious movements and expressions, decentering traditional church life and hierarchies.

In *Resurrecting Excellence*, former divinity school dean L. Gregory Jones uses the metaphor of a relay race to describe the assumptions that underlie the conventional graduate theological curriculum today.[3] In the nineteenth century, theological schools could assume that applicants had been formed as disciples of Christ by their churches and had been educated in the liberal arts at college. They could also assume that the church that had formed the candidate was still in the aspiring minister's life, supporting and even funding them. Whether the candidate would return to serve that church or not, the expectation was that graduate theological students were headed back to the church, with rare exceptions for those who would remain in the academy. Thus, the church handed the baton—represented by the ministry learner—to the college and seminary, which then handed back a Christian disciple formed for ministry to the church. That relay race sequence broke down generations ago, yet graduate theological education for ministry has only recently begun to adjust its curriculum for a new population.

Examples of the most radical forms of rethinking graduate theological school have significant implications for learning through reflective practice. Technology makes distance learning for ministry possible, which is particularly significant for older learners with multiple commitments that make relocation for seminary impractical. Distance learning enables students around the world to access seminaries within their own traditions, even if those traditions are small and have only two or three accredited institutions. The rapid improvement of educational technologies, accelerated by necessity during global pandemics or due to concerns about institutional viability, seems poised to continue to the point where few concrete arguments against its quality remain.

Distance learning for seminary often requires students to initiate internships in their home settings, with less oversight from seminaries and more options to choose from. When a student in one city "attends" graduate theological school in a setting where their faculties and deans are miles—or even time zones—away, they need more help integrating their field learning with their classroom learning. On-site supervision and reflective practices offered by their seminaries require a high level of coordination. In many cases, the only local learning a student engages in comes through theological field education and CPE.

A second emerging trend in graduate theological education is an emphasis on practice over theoretical learning. Competency-Based Education (CBE) in theological schools provides students with opportunities to earn credit for ministry experience and to build curricula in cooperation with faculty members, based on what learning needs emerge from their experiences. For those already serving in ministry roles before beginning graduate theological education, CBE provides guidance for those who might otherwise rely solely on self-directed learning, such as reading and seeking out mentors. As CBE curricula become more common, they demonstrate the benefits of beginning the learning process with lived experience, then moving from experience into deeper curiosity about the Bible, theology, Christian heritage, and ministerial practice. This approach assumes that learning from experience requires reflection, not just repetition.

New trends in seminary attendance also present challenges to reflective practice for ministry learners. Those who have spent significant time working outside of religious leadership may resist the term "supervision" and all it implies. A student who has served for twenty years in ministry before taking their first graduate school class may feel disrespected when told they must engage in reflection under the guidance of another person. They may see no need to be told what to do. This resistance is not necessarily indicative of arrogance, but rather a misunderstanding of the nature of supervised theological reflection. In this context, the supervisor is not the "boss," but rather an accountability partner who helps the learner deepen their faith and ministry practice by exploring what may have frightened, challenged, or overwhelmed them.

Lifelong and Lay Leadership Development Practices That Center Theological Reflection

When an effective leader says they learned to lead through experience, they may be telling the truth, but the preposition "through" is important to note. They did not learn from experience or because of experience, but through action, reflection, and investment of insights into new actions. Graduate professional education can provide frameworks for ongoing learning, but when change is rapid and accelerating, educators cannot predict what will be important knowledge a year after a student's graduation, let alone five years or an entire career. Therefore, paying attention to practices that foster reflection and generate insights is, for the educator, time well spent.

Furthermore, the leader who is self-aware and grounded is likely to be most effective in guiding communities through seasons of change. When they understand their own motivations, triggers, strengths, and weaknesses, they can separate their emotions from their thoughts, and their thoughts from their strategies. Reflective practice makes a leader more self-aware and grounded, and it requires disciplined practices that are not easily incorporated into a busy life, especially during difficult times. In stressful periods, reflective practice becomes more—not less—important. It provides critical distance in a crisis and prevents the leader from reacting hastily in situations requiring deliberation and wisdom.

Methods for Intentional Theological Reflection

Beyond the timeframe and bounds of formal graduate theological education, a leader can engage in reflective practices that vary in frequency and form. As relates to frequency, reflective practitioners may build a life that includes regular outlets for processing experiences. To establish a foundation for healthy reflective practices, they must choose options while in a healthy place that will stand the test of difficult times. They must select activities that foster reflection and suit their styles, often requiring some trial and error. At least one practice must involve others who, even if just occasionally, act as supervisors of reflective practice, invested in the leader's learning and flourishing

The distinction between theological reflection, or theological reflective practice, and "thinking" involves the component parts suggested by a critical incident report. As a typical starting point for theological reflection, the leader selects a critical incident from their life or work that caused surprise, sadness, confusion, anger, or any other notable reaction that sparks curiosity. They describe the incident and the feelings, ideally—but not necessarily—with a trained supervisor, and hold it up against the light of different ways of knowing: intellect, instinct, and faith. Crucially, they consider what God had to do with the event and where God might be trying to teach or show them. They gather insights and imagine how they might be reinvested in future endeavors, or at least future understanding. The critical incident report includes component parts—event, observations, investigation, insights, reinvestment—in a specific sequence that begins with an event. Many different practices either include these steps or create a healthy environment for them.

Options for reflective practices range from those leaders engage as individuals to group reflections. Individual options for reflection include journaling, visual arts, or other methods for capturing learning and gaining perspective on it. Meditation and prayer might not equate to reflective practices, depending on how the leader engages them, but they both create an internal atmosphere of awareness and readiness to face difficult questions. Similarly, embodied practices such as yoga, walking, or therapeutic massage ground the person in the moment, promoting awareness that transcends rational information gathering.

Writing for an audience or preparing a sermon can be considered theologically reflective practices that lie on the border between individual reflection and those involving a supervisor. A preacher selects a text—whether or not it comes from readings appointed in a lectionary—and assesses it for what seem like surface irregularities. As they work through what caught their attention in scripture and then communicate their findings in a sermon, they engage both in reflection and in connection with others. Similarly, when writing to constituents to inform them about important matters or to persuade them to support a strategically significant action, leaders consolidate their thoughts and not only change the minds of their readers, but also their own.

Working one-on-one with counselors, bosses, theological reflection supervisors, therapists, or spiritual directors, a leader has a space to share observations and test out their meaning-making on a routine basis. Like a personal trainer offering structure and instruction to someone seeking fitness, a competent theological reflection partner ensures that insights do not go unnoticed. Knowing that they are part of a theological reflection accountability relationship causes the leadership learner to take note when they experience the disruptions that could become material for a critical incident report.

Much like theological educators in seminaries might call theological reflection the gold standard for leadership learning, some denominational leaders consider colleague groups among religious leaders to be the gold standard for ongoing growth in reflective practice. These groups take many forms. Some are assigned and structured by denominational leaders tasked with enhancing ministers' professional effectiveness. Others are self-organized by ministers around lectionary study or case-sharing collaborations. Self-directed peer groups, without a facilitator, do well to agree on a methodology for how their time will be used. They are also wise to covenant to honor confidences, encourage reflection rather than advice-giving, and to show up authentically and vulnerably for one another.

Habits and Mentalities

Reflective practice is not a game, and its success requires a supportive environment. One of the most important attributes of that environment is a predisposition toward honesty. When leaders' inner lives are unexamined and overwhelming, their reports on what they consider "the truth" can become distorted. In other words, they may lie to constituents or deceive themselves. They may invest in easy answers and quick fixes. One benefit of accountability partners in theological reflection is that leaders can train their words and thoughts toward honesty through the continuous practice of truthful speech. As theological educator Dudley Rose would often tell students and field education supervisors, "When you're honest for one hour each week, it gets harder to lie to yourself."[4]

Another key dimension of a life conducive to reflective practice is one that values friendship. Leaders can be introverts or extroverts and still value time with people they enjoy and respect. Friends speak to each other honestly and kindly. They support one another and help each other solve problems. Taking the time to share thoughts and feelings with others also provides time for reflection. The simple act of choosing how to describe an experience to a trusted person—one who knows the leader in both good and bad times—can move someone out of crisis mode and into the process of framing an informal yet generative critical incident report. By sharing their stories, leaders listen to their own words, gaining new perspectives, even if all the friend provided was a listening ear.

Leadership pain is not pathological. A final dimension of the atmosphere a leader cultivates so that reflective practices can take root is accepting and understanding the truth that leadership is difficult and complex. Leaders find no benefit in harboring resentment toward tough times. Everyone, in every walk of life, has good days and bad days. If they expect all their days to be good, or that someone—God? Their constituents?—owes them an apology when outcomes are unexpectedly poor, they will not come at experiences with the attitude of a learner. In a culture of hyper-transparency, where every move leaders make is seen and scrutinized, leaders are bound to face criticism for their mistakes. Critique comes even when mistakes are rare, or when actions, however unpopular, were not wrong. Therefore, leaders must redouble their efforts to normalize ups and downs. Shutting down on bad days deprives them of the very substance of what they can learn about God, the world, and leadership.

Fostering Theological Reflection for Others as a Leadership Practice

Religious leaders not only grow in leadership through reflective practice over the course of their careers, but they can also foster leadership development in others by teaching and creating opportunities to engage in the practice. In his work on adult development, education and leadership scholar Robert Kegan explains how adults mature by moving from being subject to their assumptions—accepting them blindly—to becoming objective about them. This "subject–object relationship," the movement of so-called truths from blind acceptance to clear-eyed observation, is the engine that drives maturity. A leader who is continuously becoming more objective about their circumstances and less subject to unexamined assumptions does not want to leave their constituents behind. By helping those around them grow, they fulfill their ministries by helping others find fullness of life and by broadening the base of mature leaders in the community.

Options abound for engaging in leadership development for others through reflective practice models. In addition to those from which the ministerial leader can select, they can implement frameworks available through literature on leadership development. In *Spiritual Discovery: A Method for Discernment in Small Groups and Congregations*, Catherine Tran and Sandra Boyd recommend a "prayer model" for congregations developed by spiritual teacher Jane Vennard.[6] In Vennard's methodology, a prayer group assigns roles to participants: seeker, observer, timekeeper, and compassionate observer. The seeker shares a critical incident, and the others ensure that the seeker has the group's full attention. Vennard's structure prevents advice-giving or self-referential commentary, focusing instead on the seeker's experience.

In their "shared wisdom model" guide to case studies on ministerial reflective practice, theological education scholars Jeffrey Mahan, Barbara Troxell, and Carol Allen suggest that careful phasing, rather than role assignments, are key to meaningful group-based reflective practice.[7] Their suggested sequence includes the presentation of a critical incident by the sharer, clarifying questions from the group, personal and professional wisdom sharing, and a group discussion about how God's wisdom sheds light on the incident. The session concludes with two final steps: uplifting the sharer's ministry and evaluating the process.

In a culture where leaders receive praise when they solve problems and achieve a great deal quickly, but need more time to bring about meaningful change in the spiritual lives of those in their care, methodologies for reflective practice matter. They help slow leaders down and encourage listening. In their study of emergent leadership development practices, *Another Way: Living and Leading Change On-Purpose*, Stephen Lewis, Matthew Williams, and Dori Baker commend a simple acronym to guide group reflection: CARE.[8]

C: create a hospitable space.
A: ask life-giving questions.
R: reflect theologically.
E: enact a new way.

Without structure, groups are unlikely to reflect at all on their shared ministries. Too busy carrying out tasks and functioning in settings that devalue and discourage reflection, they benefit from careful agendas for reflective practice, counteracting the gravitational pull toward mere productivity.

Obstacles and Barriers to Reflective Practice

Obsession with productivity, devaluing of depth of thought and character, and privileging action over reflection are just a few of the many obstacles to dedicating time and attention to reflective practice. Leaders often hear, "Why do you need to psychoanalyze everything? Just do it!" Ministerial leaders are expected to devote their attention to business and legal matters daily, but when they seek to persuade those trained in law and business to engage in theological reflection, their efforts are not taken seriously. Due to the many barriers, ministerial leadership learners must approach reflective practice—both their own and the practice they seek to foster in their constituents—with determination and zeal.

Zeal follows from understanding the countercultural nature of reflective practice. The same scholar who introduced the concept of the "subject–object relationship" as a driver of maturity, Robert Kegan, also developed the theoretical framework, "Immunity to Change."[9] He and his colleague, Lisa Lahey, explain that when an adult learner encounters an internal obstacle to life-giving change, they must uncover the competing commitment preventing their growth. For instance, someone trying to improve their punctuality must understand what's keeping them from being on time. Only by identifying and challenging this competing commitment can they develop better habits.

What keeps leaders from engaging in reflective practice? First, they believe leadership learning through experience should happen effortlessly as they go through life, with no intentionality. When respected scholars and educators do not require learners to engage in a practice, they convey a message that what was not required was also not important. When professionals do not see evidence of reflective practice as a common undertaking, they think it does not matter.

Second, leaders experience cognitive dissonance when they encounter difficulties they believe are unique to them. They feel alone and confused when people dislike them for unfair reasons, when they are not respected the way their predecessors were respected for merely showing up, and when they hear feedback that they are bad at a task at which they previously believed themselves to be good. Cognitive dissonance does not foster curiosity for those who feel insecure, and most new leaders are insecure. Popular culture suggests that leaders should be fully prepared and utterly perfect, otherwise they deserve any harsh criticism. When leaders realize that they actually have a great deal to learn, and that the challenges they face have no history from which they can glean instruction, they may want to hide their incompetence rather than use it as an opportunity to learn.

Third, basic conversational skills—once a normal part of thoughtful dialogue—can no longer be taken for granted. Technology connects people through short bursts of information, creating the illusion of engagement when it is often just exchanging announcements. In her book *Conversation: A Sacred Art*, Diane Millis explores how meaningful conversations can deepen relationships and self-awareness.[10] Without strong conversational skills, diving into a discussion of a critical incident filled with hard truths isn't a realistic first step. If leadership and ministry require people skills, and conversation is one such skill, the superficial nature of modern interactions presents a significant challenge for reflective practitioners.

Conclusion

The resurrected Christ made himself known to his followers through dialogue about a critical incident they had experienced:

> Now on that same day [that the women found the empty tomb and heard from the angel that Jesus had risen] two [of Jesus's followers] were going to a village called Emmaus, about seven miles from Jerusalem, and talking with each other about all these things that had happened. While they were talking and discussing, Jesus himself came near and went with them, but their eyes were kept from recognizing him. And he said to them, "What are you discussing with each other while you walk along?" They stood still, looking sad. Then one of them, whose name was Cleopas, answered him, "Are you the only stranger in Jerusalem who does not know the things that have taken place there in these days?" He asked them, "What things?" — Luke 24:13–19a

Jesus shows interest in the lived experience of those who followed the news of his ministry and execution and asks the question reflective practitioners raise about the most challenging and meaningful things they experience: "What things?"

Leadership learning begins with self-awareness. A lifelong, intentional practice of theological reflection benefits both leaders and the communities they serve. Self-aware leaders are more likely to set appropriate boundaries, make thoughtful decisions, and model behaviors that inspire others to do the same. Leaders who treat every experience as an opportunity for learning are less likely to find their work mundane and more likely to approach their challenges with curiosity and wonder. When viewed as material for reflection, even a leader's worst moments can become critical incidents that lead to the discovery of light and truth. Even the roughest experiences can become gateways to deeper knowledge, or even revelation.

CHAPTER SIX

Leadership Development Through Expanding Horizons

January, 2023

"Cora" walked JJ and me over to the classroom we were going to spend the next two weeks painting. She showed us, within reason, what her hopes were. She wanted cheerful colors, a sense of order, and otherwise wanted us to handle the project however we wanted.

However we wanted?

JJ is twenty, and I'm her fifty-something-year-old mother. We are volunteering at a children's home in Peru. JJ spent her first eleven months in a setting not unlike this one, but in China. She is now on a gap year before college, traveling all around the world. This leg of her journey is the one on which I chose to tag along, based on the timing, though many details about the trip changed after I first agreed to partner with her in Peru.

First, we changed our location. Initially, JJ had us set up to volunteer on a farm in an adjacent region. Somehow, accidentally, we bought airline tickets to the wrong city. As the crow flies, the two cities in question looked close-by to one another, but there is a little something lying between them called the Andes. We tried everything we could think of to get from our selected airport to the farm. Ultimately, our hosts there ghosted us when they got annoyed by our questions about transport. The great irony is that they posted negatively about JJ on a volunteer website because we asked so many questions and left them in the lurch when we canceled. How they thought we would get across a mountain range to them without answering our questions... Well, no one ever said that international volunteering was easy.

We resolved issue number one with the help of God. God, who never abandons; God, who does not allow even our own cluelessness to separate us from that which is life-giving and good; God, who thought my attempting to farm was already questionable before the whole transport-over-mountains-into-jungle problem.

Desperate for a Plan B, I googled "volunteer opportunities" in the city where our flight would take us. I found a children's home for children whose parents cannot take care of them, now or maybe ever. I called the phone number, and the executive director, John, picked up on the first ring. By the time I hung up, we had a volunteer gig, a place to stay with meals included, and a ride to and from the airport.

The second obstacle has turned out to be a nonissue, at least so far. Peru's president is currently in jail after trying to disband the congress. Protestors are shutting down some roads and airports, and hundreds of travelers were recently stranded in Cusco, where the Machu Picchu ruins attract tourists from all over the world. Both my mother and one of my best friends reached out with the question: Are you still going to go? We got advice from both our host John and my best friend Shannon, who works in Latin American affairs, that the north—where the children's home is located—has been untouched by protests or other disruptions. We were not even flying through Lima, so JJ and I never seriously considered canceling. [n.b. JJ's travels were disrupted due to the protests, but she rescheduled her Machu Picchu trip for another time.]

The reason I chose to say yes to this trip was not that JJ wanted company. In fact, I rather had to invite myself along. I pushed myself to do this. When plans were coming together, I had just contracted with a publisher to write a book on leadership development for ministers and other communal leaders, and I knew I would need a project like this one to make an honest writer of me. I had to engage in some leadership learning that did not feel easy or comfortable, as I knew I would be making the argument that one key dimension of leadership learning was to get comfortable with being uncomfortable.

Leadership does not come easier to me than it does to anyone else; I just prefer the dis-ease of leadership to boredom. I am no less conflict-averse than anyone else; I just can't stand walking on eggshells. These two dimensions of my leadership personality have helped me to face the uncomfortable in my work as dean of a tradition-specific seminary, embedded in an ecumenical divinity school, which has relocated and merged with a university divinity school on my watch.

I am literally never bored at work because I find myself in over my head regularly, tasked with projects for which I have had no training. The kinds of conflicts I have been called upon to address have professional life-and-death impacts on people I care about. I have faced challenges at the outermost edges of my competence, ranging from learning new technology to trying new media for writing to responsibilities that deeply and immutably affect people and institutions entrusted to my care. Examples of such high-stakes administrative responsibilities have included managing legal negotiations involving laws I did not know existed, and counseling students through crises that had no name when I was at their phase of life—all while seeking to embody the non-anxious presence that instills confidence in others regarding my competence to lead them.

I work in adult education and attend workshops and continuing education classes for fun. Many I encounter in such settings find work outside their expertise to be exhausting, and continuing education for leadership to be soul-crushing in its failure to meet their needs. This is not, mind you, a problem with learners. The fact is that most leadership training—workshops, courses, reading—engages only a sliver of learning styles; I just happen to live in that sliver. I needed to push myself outside that comfort zone because I am about to tell readers how and why they must do the same to learn to be more effective leaders.

Therefore, I came to Peru to do something I have never done before and to be reminded what it feels like to be a beginner in every way. My Spanish is limited, although I can get by with patience on the part of my conversation partners. I have not painted much, but I am methodical, careful, and unafraid to ask for help, so I do not think I will make a terrible mess of things. I am aware of my surroundings, using the buddy system with my young-adult daughter, and serving in a setting that seems hospitable so far. Therefore, I have controlled for the variables that could have tipped the scales from risky to foolish. Now, I just need to let go of my need to know what I am doing, my desire to know exactly what will happen next, and my fears of not being liked. If those are my biggest risks, I am hopeful I will learn a great deal.

Leadership at the Edge of Competence

Communal leadership today can overwhelm even the smartest, bravest, and most strategic professionals, volunteers, and heads of households due to its sheer interdisciplinarity. To lead an organization, community, or family, those in charge must embody many roles: visionary, manager, human resources coordinator, justice advocate, technology specialist, financial analyst, fundraiser, aesthete, nutritionist, first responder, journalist, social worker, therapist, advocate, instructor, and archivist.

Professional development must become as multidisciplinary as the work of leadership, yet there is too much to be known for any offering to encompass all that a leader might confront. This is especially true in rapidly changing times when the problems of tomorrow are unknown today. Therefore, useful learning comes in the form of opportunities to function well amidst uncertainty and novelty. Such opportunities simulate today's leadership environment, where new issues emerge daily, demanding the leader's attention and intervention. When a person takes on something new, they feel incompetent. Only through engagement, trial, error, and practice can they move from that feeling of incompetence into confidence—though not hubris—and get things done.

Horizon expansion is the intentional practice of placing oneself in a situation that is bound to be uncomfortable for the sake of growth. A person's horizon is only as wide as the range of their comfort zones, and those with too narrow a comfort zone find leadership in uncertain times terrifying. The benefits of stretching beyond what feels easy spill over from one experience into another: Overcoming a fear of heights can reduce social anxiety, and trying new foods can increase a person's willingness to travel to destinations unknown. As part of a repertoire of leadership development undertakings, horizon expansion builds capacity for tolerating the anxiety that accompanies new content and new self-knowledge.

Leadership development through horizon expansion is more important in a time when professions, and the context in which they function, are changing quickly. Horizon-expanding experiences foster humility in the face of what a person does not know or understand. When a person tries something new, no one can rightly shame them for their inexpert incompetence. When accustomed to the feeling of being a novice, unskilled, leaders realize that such feelings are normal and nothing to be embarrassed about.

Furthermore, those who are comfortable with being uncomfortable are less likely to engage in avoidant behavior. Bad leadership habits, such as chronic procrastination, improve when leaders get used to the difficult feelings of being out of their depth and come to understand them as normal, not threatening. Leaders who avoid unpleasant tasks—such as conflict, hard truths, and disappointing others—do so at the peril of their effectiveness. Horizon expansion functions like exposure therapy for those seeking to overcome irrational fears, building up the individual's tolerance for discomfort and their confidence that they can survive.

The Benefits and Ethics of Horizon Expansion

"Mansplaining" entered popular cultural language in the early 2020s. The term refers to unsolicited lessons offered by men, usually to women, regarding topics with which the audience is already familiar. Mansplainers are either arrogant about how much they know or insecure about how little they know, and patronizing those they perceive to have less knowledge either satisfies their egos or relieves their anxiety. Leadership development through horizon expansion reduces these mansplaining impulses. It does so by normalizing unfamiliarity for those who are afraid others will see their ignorance.

Stretching beyond comfort zones also increases a leader's humility and curiosity, causing them to ask more questions rather than impose unwanted answers as a power play. Those who regularly engage in challenging and new activities shake off their need to appear knowledgeable, discover gifts in themselves, and experience wonder at the gifts of others. Their new experiences evoke emotions like fear, joy, and satisfaction, broadening their emotional range.

Horizon expansion can help a person overcome character flaws that irritate those around them and the people they lead. A person who is open, with an expansive view of the world, is less likely to condescend to or underestimate others. They are quicker to trust because they have experienced moments where they had to relinquish the role of "expert" in favor of the identity of "beginner." Upon realizing that momentary dependence brought them excitement and adventure, they become less afraid to let go of control in other settings.

The problem that can counterbalance the benefits of horizon expansion is that a leader who engages in it might overcome one form of self-centeredness only to embrace another. Many activities associated with expanding horizons instrumentalize "the other." In cultivating a lifelong leadership development practice, the leader must consider carefully whether they are learning at the expense of others, causing psychological harm or physical deprivation, or placing themselves or those responsible for them in physical danger. They must also be aware of the natural tendency to judge others whose horizons they deem too narrow.

Balanced, healthy, and self-aware practices for expanding horizons are possible through intentionality. A well-curated self-development protocol should include both horizon-expanding experiences and thoughtful, ethical critique of those experiences. When combined with content learning and reflective practice, the benefits of building a capacity for wonder and openness are too valuable to dismiss, especially when effort can address potential drawbacks.

Educational, Theological, and Developmental Perspectives on Horizon-Expanding Leadership Development

Among those who study adult learning, Jack Mezirow ranks as the parent of the field now called "education for transformation." Mezirow writes that education does not begin with the transmission of factual information or self-awareness, but rather with what he calls a "disorienting dilemma." It is only through reorientation that a learner can come to terms with the assumptions the dilemma upended, revealing their insufficiency, and showing that assumptions were never the learner's true ally. The phases of learning Mezirow presents include a disorienting dilemma, self-examination, critical assessment of assumptions, recognition that others have experienced similar disorientation, and reintegration.[1]

In his work on theologically reflective practice, Kenneth Pohly also names disorientation—"rough places"[2]—as the proper starting point for learning. From a theological perspective, new questions emerge regarding how the leader might ethically identify and enter the right rough places for learning. A particularly Christian ethical approach requires that learners predicate their horizon-expansion efforts on *agape*: love for self and others. They do not believe that they smooth off their rough edges through sheer humanistic willpower. Instead, they believe that God is actively invested in smoothing those rough edges while minimizing harm to God's beloved.

That God would not call a leader into horizon expansion that causes harm to the vulnerable or instrumentalizes others for the leader's benefit is self-evident. Less obvious are the implications of God's love for the learner seeking growth. Many practices aimed at growing comfort zones involve suffering, some of which may be edifying. However, some growth practices may reflect a striving for self-improvement rooted in self-loathing. An Ironman Triathlon is likely to expand a person's horizons through overcoming physical pain and limitations. Competing while ill or injured, however, might betray a lack of respect for one's God-given body. The Christian leader seeking a wider comfort zone must ground their striving in love for themselves, love for others, and wonder at God's creation. Seeking to grow through self-punishment reinforces the self-centeredness that horizon expansion is meant to overcome.

Decentering

The theological moves that horizon expansion facilitates in an adult's development include decentering, welcoming, and uprooting. Decentering the self in favor of a broader worldview constitutes an inner shift in perspective that benefits both individuals and the communities around them. Babies obsess over their own needs because their mind's developmental capacity allows them to do that and nothing else. They cry out to have those needs met and are unready to acknowledge the needs of others, including those of their caregivers and others with whom they share the world. As toddlers, they begin to learn that other people are just that: *other people.*

Over the course of a lifetime, healthy human beings move from the utter centralization of their needs to utter concern for others, including those who will come after them. Few adults possess pure and perfect emotional health, however. Life's anxiety-provoking traumas scare people at various crossroads into thinking their needs require a return to obsessive self-protection. The one whose heart has been broken through lost love, for example, might become self-absorbed for a season or an era of their lives, losing track of the hurts and heartbreaks of others as they conserve energy for their own healing.

Those whose development toward agapistic love for others, as well as themselves, has been interrupted can train their minds through horizon-expanding self-development. They can get back on track toward decentering themselves through exposure to and investment in the needs of other people. Decentering thus paves the way to, and is a prerequisite for, expanded horizons.

Welcoming

Spiritual teacher Father Thomas Keating[3] taught those seeking spiritual direction from him the practice of "centering prayer." This form of meditative prayer suited those seeking a deeper relationship with God beyond worship and even beyond words. The practice calls a praying person to select—or allow to bubble up—a spiritually meaningful word (such as "peace," "love," or "grace") and then meditate on it for twenty minutes, twice daily, morning and evening. Much like breath meditation in various faiths, when the prayerful person's attention strays, as it inevitably will, they are taught to return to their sacred word. Practitioners who engage in centering prayer often describe a sense of groundedness in God, discovering mental clarity and a capacity to keep adversity in perspective.

Keating's students, however, expressed a need for practices to rely on during times of busyness and distraction as well. In response to that feedback, Keating developed "welcoming prayer," the active corollary to centering prayer. Like many dimensions of Jesuit spirituality, welcoming prayer relies on embodied knowledge. Jesuits describe the body as the repository of the subconscious, where feelings correspond to specific bodily locations. Welcoming prayer encourages awareness and acceptance of bodily sensations, rather than falling into the humanistic trap of disregarding the incarnate in favor of the lofty abstract.

Welcoming prayer is intended to be a practice in real time, not just within a meditation session. When encountering adversity, the individual first identifies where in their body they sense the adversity and sinks into that location and feeling. They say, "Welcome," allowing the feeling rooted in a bodily location to act as a communicator, rather than as a problem to be solved. After sinking into and welcoming the feeling, the person engaging in a welcoming prayer follows a series of four releases, each corresponding to a vestigial childhood anxiety that no longer serves a meaningful purpose. They say to themselves:

1. I release my need for power and control.
2. I release my need for safety and security.
3. I release my need for love and esteem.
4. I release my need to change any of this.

Afterward, they continue with their day, not resisting their body's messages but also not succumbing to unhelpful anxieties. Like centering prayer, welcoming prayer grounds the individual, making them less subject to worries both old and new.

Uprooting

The learner who has decentered themselves and come to terms with the vestigial anxieties carried from childhood into adulthood is ready to manage life and leadership without a safety net. Becoming aware of one's own assumptions and location in the world can be unsettling, and this process unfolds gradually rather than in a single moment. Ultimately, the individual who is comfortable with not being at the center of the universe, and not tethered to illusions of control, is prepared to thrive without clinging to symbols of security. Such a person is no longer rooted in a specific source of comfort but can find what they need at different way stations along the journey.

Some uproot certain assumptions only to re-root themselves in others. Others manage to detach from assumptions entirely, opening themselves up to new possibilities for themselves and their communities. The purpose of consistent horizon expansion is to maintain rootedness in God and God alone, independent of specific circumstances. The person who decenters, welcomes, and uproots does not inure themselves to discomfort but instead comes to understand that discomfort is not dangerous in itself; in fact, it promotes wakefulness. This person, therefore, becomes comfortable with discomfort as a natural part of being fully present to the needs of the world.

Leaders who claim that adversity gave them a "thick skin" may mean two different things. Some leaders become calloused and numb after facing down critics, failures, and enemies. Others, however, realize that seeking approval, popularity, or saying only what their constituents want to hear is not worth the cost of losing integrity. Experience helps either way, as do curated examples of successes and failures from which a leader can learn. The ideal to which leaders strive should not be developing thicker skin or building higher walls, but instead cultivating a deeper sense of rootedness in ultimate truth.

Horizon-Expanding Practice for Transformational Leadership Learning

With all the benefits, ethical considerations, and potential drawbacks of horizon expansion for leadership development, what are the practical activities leaders undertake to achieve it? Previous chapters explored how leaders can become more knowledgeable about their fields and their inner lives. Horizon expansion requires leaders to operate at the edge of their comfort zones, becoming more confident and relaxed in the face novelty and potential fear. Examples below of various horizon-expansion practices might seem harmless to a healthy person, yet they can threaten those who are rooted in their assumptions and attached to their illusions of control.

Relationships, Especially Relationships Across Differences

In her writings about conversation as a sacred art, Diane Millis suggests that conversation can be a faith practice like any other.[4] Conversation fosters closeness between people and simultaneously with God, working dialectically rather than iteratively. In an iterative exchange, one person shares, the other person shares, and each receives information as a trade.

Dialectical relationships, however, cause both participants to change: One shares a story, and in the sharing, they are transformed; the listener is also transformed, and what they share in return shapes them further. Conversation thus expands knowledge of the self, the other, and all creation.

One term that describes the growth in awareness that occurs in such relationships of deep sharing is "diacognition."[5] This term encompasses dialogue (conversation), cognition (awareness), and position (contextual positionality, or cultural proprioception). When two or more people form a relationship across differences and share stories about their lives, their horizons expand as they gain new perspectives on the world through each other's experiences. When conversation deepens into a relationship, it fosters not only decentering, welcoming, and uprooting, but also a greater capacity for love and empathy.

Diacognition, as a multivalent sense, builds capacity for other kinds of learning but also requires ethical critique. When two people from different backgrounds connect, one is almost certainly going to hold a position of power over the other in certain ways. A person with privilege risks exoticizing or instrumentalizing the person with less privilege, especially when that conversation partner's stories include suffering or want. True conversation has no agenda, yet few conversations in real life are completely devoid of any personal gain or goal.

Despite such critiques, horizon expansion through relationship, particularly those across differences, is a worthy undertaking. When grounded in the singular agenda—telling the truth to each other with hopes of mutual transformation—and carried out with care regarding power dynamics, dialogue is the acorn capable of growing into a mighty oak. In her metaphorical references to fractals, adrienne maree brown suggests that "small is all"—a reflection of how every part of a system can reflect the whole.[6]

Relationships, particularly between people separate from each other yet having much in common, can do more to foster change than may initially seem possible. These dyads, or conversations between two people, by their very existence, can catalyze transformation in the larger, fractured whole.

Volunteer Service

Many organizations that care about education for transformation employ the pedagogical tools of service learning. Schools and professional settings find horizon-expansion in volunteer service in settings that have a need to be fulfilled through work. High schools and colleges might provide volunteer opportunities to their students to help them to gain perspective and experience. Businesses, such as the consulting firm Accenture, offer "stretch opportunities"[7] for employee career development. Volunteer opportunities appear to increase retention at Accenture, as employees find meaning and fulfillment in service.

Volunteerism comes with a shadow side, like ethical concerns regarding power differentials, and people with privilege instrumentalizing those with less privilege to advance their own learning. Corporation board members might be pleased to hear that volunteerism increases productivity, but they would surely be less pleased if volunteerism were to take time away from money-making endeavors. For younger people, episodic forays into volunteerism could send the message that care for those less fortunate is just a box to check, while reinforcing barriers between social classes in other areas of life.

These ethical puzzles might lead some to dismiss service learning, given the many slippery slopes on it presents. However, this would be an overreaction, especially considering the transformational possibilities associated with learning through serving disadvantaged communities. Volunteering across cultural, geographical, and ethnic differences fosters a sense of global citizenship and social connectedness with others. Although these outcomes might not result for everyone or from every experience, learning how interconnected all creation truly is can make service learning a valuable form of lifelong leadership education. The scale and complexity of the world's problems are daunting, so forming citizens who are willing to engage with these issues is a high priority,[8] despite the risks and downsides that can be managed by thoughtful educators.

Volunteer service across difference is not solely the purview of the privileged, but privilege often provides the time and economic flexibility that makes volunteering possible. This class differential is not an argument against learning through volunteering, but it must be acknowledged and addressed. "Pedagogy of the privileged" is an emerging area of adult education scholarship, where scholars consider how privilege can be examined, leveraged, and mobilized. This pedagogy is not about teaching people how to hold on to power but of framing transformational education that helps everyone understand the power they wield, the power others have over them, and how to foster a more egalitarian and democratic society. Those who have privilege and never become aware of it may not only fail to serve others due to a misguided sense of deserving everything they have, but they also fall prey to temptations to oppress disadvantaged groups by pitting them against each other.

Though it may seem controversial, especially given the fact that those with privilege already have access to ample educational opportunities, pedagogy of the privileged recognizes that everyone is privileged in some way. For example, a male-bodied person from a low-income background holds advantages over female- or queer-bodied individuals from the same environment. Similarly, an able-bodied woman has advantages over those with disabilities. Along various intersections of identity, people hold both advantages and disadvantages, justifying the need for a specific pedagogy of privilege. Almost anyone could benefit from examining their privileges, as unexamined advantages are almost always misused.

In her work on the pedagogy of the privileged, which she calls an understudied area, education scholar Ann Curry-Stevens charts out the following phases of discovery that can be fostered through pedagogy of the privileged:

1. Confidence shaking
2. Awareness of oppression
3. Locating oneself as oppressed
4. Locating oneself as privileged
5. Understanding the benefits that flow from privilege

6. Understanding oneself as implicated in the oppression of others
7. Confidence building
8. Planning action
9. Finding community for sustained growth
10. Declaring intention for future actions[9]

When arguing that volunteer service expands the learner's horizons, these ten steps serve as an important reminder that—much like theological reflection described in the previous chapter—service itself is not sufficient for transformation. It is not the work, but the reflection on the work, that brings about change. Of course, reflection can happen on the part of an individual, but transformational education also requires structure and accountability.

Travel

Travel, in all its forms, can expand the traveler's horizons. A trip that involves seeing friends and family deepens relationships and provides opportunities for conversation despite differences. A vacation built solely around relaxation makes space for reflective practice. As a method for lifelong learning for leadership, travel transcends many different educational strategies in its inherent interdisciplinarity and capacity to transform.[10] The body's outer journey through travel experiences an inner journey that blends religious studies, philosophy, psychology, sociology, anthropology, and geography, as well as other sources such as history, literature, and biography. It also includes transrational dimensions, such as knowing through being in an unfamiliar space via cultural osmosis.[11]

In an article entitled, "Journeys into Transformation: Travel to an 'Other' Place as a Vehicle of Transformation," education scholar Alun Morgan argues that a traveler who undertakes a journey with a strong ethical framework, including a code of conduct that insists they do no harm, can protect those who call the traveler's destination home. That code should include a promise on the part of the traveler to focus on commonality over otherness, since romanticizing otherness risks exoticizing difference and reinforcing power differentials.[12]

In her book *Beyond Guilt Trips: Mindful Travel in an Unequal World*, Anu Taranath argues that power differentials are a sufficient justification for why learning through travel is important. She writes that the world is hierarchical and structurally unequal, requiring leaders who can talk meaningfully about difficult topics like slavery, imperialism, colonialism, and disparities of wealth and opportunity.[13] Travel provides a language for dialogue that helps leaders to grow and helps them cultivate growth in the communities they serve. To "boldly notice" differences,[14] and learn to talk about them, helps the traveler understand how they fit into systems bigger than themselves, systems in which they have the capacity to effect change.

Taranath argues that learners should by no means avoid travel to underprivileged lands, nor should they feel guilty while there. She recommends that the traveler, when feeling uncomfortable and tempted to recoil, should focus on staying present and building relationships.[15] Guilt is counterproductive, she argues, if it prevents the traveler from engaging with people and places, differences and similarities. Guilt comes with self-focus, even self-pity, and self-focus diminishes the traveler's awareness of the world around them.[16]

Ironically, one of the reasons why travel to less wealthy lands is possible is because past colonization and environmental degradation made it inexpensive, as some travel destinations have become dependent on tourism.[17] Amid such complexities, the learner encounters two coexisting truths that they might never fully reconcile: They did not create inequality, but they are embedded in it.[18] In those truths' irreconcilability, the learner's mental work increases their empathy.[19] Travel brings up many powerful feelings for the traveler,[20] just as volunteer service does for the volunteer. With a strong facilitator to debrief travel experiences[21] and an ethical framework guiding engagement, travel can correct for the worst harms while preserving its tremendous learning opportunities.

Able facilitators take responsibility for upholding ethical frameworks for travel amid power differentials, demonstrate empathy for travelers experiencing strong emotions, and model relationship-building over recoil and avoidance. Whether coordinating a schedule, managing partnerships on the ground in the faraway place, or organizing preparatory and debriefing dialogue sessions, the facilitator maintains awareness of the journey as a learning opportunity. The traveler can self-facilitate through intentional practices for fostering awareness, such as journaling, choosing a broad range of settings to visit (not just the tourist destinations but settings where life is lived), and talking to strangers with warmth and an open mind.

Mixing and Matching Practices for Horizon Expansion

Combining horizon-expanding educational interventions can increase the impact of learning experiences on learners. A combination that many adult learners, from college students to churchgoers, recognize as important is the blending of travel and volunteerism. In a study on the effects of volunteer tourism on a group of learners from Brazil, scholars identified the challenges participants faced: adverse conditions, unusual situations, and culture shock. These three opportunities for horizon expansion all have relevance to leadership development, which requires a shift in perspective every time the leader encounters something new. Add to those benefits the learning that takes place within a group of volunteers, such as learning how to resolve conflicts and how not to jump to conclusions, and the benefits become even clearer.[22]

Ethical practices for volunteering in unfamiliar spaces deserve attention and care because they make such experiences possible. Without them, the better course of action would be to leave settings well enough alone. The growth potential of such service is so worthwhile that it justifies the effort required to attend to power differentials and the protection of the vulnerable. The purpose of expanding horizons is to normalize the feelings of discomfort associated with unfamiliarity, inexpert knowledge, and loss of control. The discomfort should apply only to the learner, who has chosen to place themselves in unfamiliar territory. It should come at negligible cost to those in the setting where learning takes place, or to the setting itself.

To curate meaningful horizon-expanding experiences, the learner must seek out experiences that take them outside their comfort zones. While the learner might assume that such experiences must be dramatic—skydiving, rock climbing, rugged international travel—most people's horizons are narrow. Therefore, a range of blended practices can achieve the desired results of becoming comfortable with the discomfort that comes with the new and unfamiliar.

Unfamiliar forms of self-care can stretch the learner to know the world and themselves better. Yoga literally stretches the body and figuratively stretches the mind. Those who practice it learn about balance and inner peace, but even the most experienced yogis do not claim to be experts with nothing left to learn. Martial arts and dance require the beginner to set aside their egos, but not their self-esteem. They find confidence despite their newness and literal incompetence, as they can take heart in the fact that they are capable of trying and growing. If a learner can risk appearing inadequate and find that only good comes of it, they are more likely to take risks that further their objectives in other parts of their lives without undue anxiety.

Hobbies also expand the learner's horizons. Practicing a hobby that has nothing to do with workplace productivity sharpens thinking and simulates the ongoing process of developing mastery. Hobbies provide low-risk simulations of project completion, giving the learner opportunities to stretch that do not immediately affect others. The artist might try a hundred different combinations of blue and red to make purple for a canvas, seeking the color that is just right. Doing so costs nothing for an institution or community waiting on the leader for direction, but the leader has the opportunity to refine their taste and revel in the freedom to explore before returning to settings of accountability to a mission.

Reading and pursuing courses of study might be practices most closely associated with staying up to date in a field. However, reading beyond their field expands the leader's horizons. The faith community leader might read about the practice of ministry to grow in knowledge to invest in their communities, but then read science fiction to expand their imagination. The professor who takes a course at their university every semester in the field remotest from the one in which they teach and research grows in empathy for students and courage to try new things in the classroom and in their scholarly pursuits.

Conclusion

The purpose of learning for horizon expansion is to increase the learner's capacity. In order to take in new content, learners must create space in their intellect and imagination for that which challenges previously held assumptions. They also must become desensitized to the natural discomforts that accompany feeling like a novice, dependent on others to show the way. Without practices that expand horizons, new content might not have room to take root, and reflective practice might only confirm what the learner thinks they already know.

Many combinations of experiences can increase the leader's capacity: travel combined with volunteering, studying a new language and reading poetry in it, taking a course on how to create a form of art and then creating it. Leaders who find themselves in a rut, where creativity is unavailable to them and discouragement abounds, need not look far to find sanctuary in spaces where their minds can roam.

The connection between horizon expansion and leadership learning might seem far-fetched, rendering such practices "extra" or "selfish." Today, perspectives like these, which devalue horizon expansion, run counter to the leader's potential for effectiveness. The leader who faces challenges never seen before must have the ability to address and embrace newness. The willingness to walk undaunted into the breach has become a basic qualification for leadership.

Part III

Integration and Improvisation

Blending Practices for Leadership Development

CHAPTER SEVEN

A Vision for the Ministry of Leadership Development

COMMUNAL LEADERSHIP, PARTICULARLY faith community leadership, has become more demanding and complicated in the early twenty-first century. The magnitude of the problems humanity faces, the diversity within communities that reduces the predictability on which leaders once relied, and the instantaneous action technology enables and demands all swirl together into a leadership context of constant churn. Furthermore, the pace of change is accelerating with each passing day, so the learning a person might undertake now for the sake of their leadership competence might not help them tomorrow.

One appropriate response to such patterns and trends is to devote more time, energy, attention, and resources to leadership development. Leaders hear that counsel so often, but only rarely is it followed by specific instructions for a realistic course of action. In a complex time, commitment to leadership development must be accompanied by a plan, yet leadership development means different things to different people.

Now is a time when all who lead must take up the cause of developing the leaders around them. All citizens must contribute to their communities in order to make their way through an uncertain time for the world. In such a season, vague assertions about what leadership development is, does, and requires are no longer useful. Those who lead with wonder and wherewithal, rather than apathy or abdication, need more than "oughts" when it comes to leadership development. They need concrete proposals for how they might undertake leadership development, and those proposals must be both realistic and sustainable over the long haul.

The future of leadership must be different from even its most recent past. The expectation that leadership skills result from the combination of strong character and passive absorption of observed behaviors has become unrealistic, if it ever really worked. The threefold, intersecting practices of accumulating content-based knowledge, reflecting theologically on leadership experiences, and intentionally broadening the horizons of one or many leaders come together to provide a framework for leadership development. This trefoil's implications for practice apply to individuals, team leaders, organizations, and evaluators of the effectiveness of all of the above.

Implications for Practice

At the installation of a graduate of the seminary I serve, I took a picture of the clergy who lined up to process into the celebration of a new ministry. As I looked down the line, I noticed that three out of four of those attending the service had graduated from my school, but it is unlikely any of them would have studied there if they were starting out on their theological education journey now. Our school was a freestanding graduate school for future ministers until 2016. Due to an array of factors—enrollment decline, physical plant deterioration, rising costs, squeamish donors, and soaring student debt—independence was not sustainable.

Our school became an embedded unit within a divinity school at a premier, world-class university. Making this change made it possible to continue our mission to educate ministers, but it also narrowed the field of who could learn with us to include those who were both extremely able academically and who could uproot and relocate for graduate school. Those who come to our school now receive full-tuition scholarships, and even stipends for living costs, but those who want to blend seminary with work and demanding family commitments cannot always make it work.

During the same years since our school relocated and affiliated, virtually all other schools in our ecclesial family have created either fully online or low-residency programs. Among our two key partner traditions, we are the only school that remains predominantly residential. Therefore, options are available for those who want to remain where they are and pursue theological education—options that were unthinkable in the twentieth century. Yet, looking at that picture, I felt a pang, and a question arose: where will tomorrow's leaders come from? Rather than dwell in that moment of worry, which could easily turn to despair for one who loves the church as it is and could be, I turned back to the question that drives me: How are the leaders of the future going to learn, over the course of a lifetime, to lead well?

A threefold set of leadership development practices—content transmission, theological reflection on lived experience, and horizon expansion—can serve as a template for a leadership development program in a wide variety of contexts and settings. The model does not rely on a specific form of power dynamics or hierarchy. It can be adopted by a team just as easily as it can be imposed by one with authority. What follows are examples of how the trefoil model might be used as a guide by individuals and groups.

One Leader Building a Strong Team Around Them

As dean of a seminary, I work with numerous constituent groups and coordinate their interaction with one another. Our school's Advisory Council, affiliated faculty, senior staff, student leaders, and fellows-at-large all care deeply about the school's mission, and it is my job to keep them engaged in the work of building up our institution. I have learned a great deal from our Advisory Council's chair about how a trefoil approach to leadership development can cause members to grow in their commitment and give of their gifts most effectively.

Every year under this chair's leadership, I have been asked to identify a theme for the year related to the most important issues the school faces. This year, I suggested a deep dive into the ways in which the significance of ordination and denominations is changing in the lives of the students we educate. Our chair asked me to write a prospectus for the topic that included several activities. In the end, leadership development activities included:

- A religious history tour of the Yale University campus, where our seminary is embedded, led by a guide who pointed out how religion in New England has both changed and remained the same over the centuries.
- One forty-five-minute session during a meeting, where Council members broke into groups and shared their own histories of affiliation with their denomination and how their affinities had changed or remained the same over their lifetimes.
- A session where Advisory Council members read articles about demographic trends, including religious switching among traditions and the rise of those who identify as spiritual but religiously unaffiliated.
- A session with a student leader who explained why, in his observation, students still care about ordination but are less tied to specific authorizing denominational bodies.

The series culminated in a white paper, written by me, that captured the Advisory Council's learning over the course of the year and defined some implications for the future.

This leadership development theme prevented the Advisory Council from descending into the weeds. Without a disciplined approach to growing in their familiarity with the key issues the school faces, they might have either disengaged or micromanaged. Instead, they learned new content about denominational and ordination trends, reflected on their own attitudes toward their faith traditions, and became more aware of their surroundings' history through an eye-opening journey across the campus.

In describing this leadership development protocol, I can see that it probably included insufficient attention to reflection and horizon expansion and a surplus of content sharing. I can point that out to our chairperson going into the new year and correct it. The trefoil can provide guidance for creating a leadership development protocol, serve as an evaluation tool for assessing the protocol, and remind us not to allow leadership development to be overly attuned to just one dimension of what a leader needs.

Curriculum Assessment and Redevelopment

I joined the faculty of Andover Newton in 2005 as the Director of Field Education and Assistant Professor of Ministerial Leadership. My appointment surprised many, as the school had offered a doctoral concentration in supervised ministries for some time, so naturally, some expected that the school would recruit from within its pool of graduates. That I was brought in from the outside indicated an overarching hope and expectation that I would bring about change.

The specific area that I identified quickly as requiring a reset was the course that accompanied students' internship year, known at the time as "Practicum." Practicum groups included seven or eight students and a discussion leader with extensive supervision training. One set of groups met in the daytime, the other in the evening. All signals pointed to a program in need of revision.

Typical student evaluations for courses at Andover Newton indicated that students were 90 percent satisfied or more, but Practicum evaluations showed 50 percent or fewer students satisfied with the course. Written comments about Practicum were negative to the point of hostility. Focus groups with students made it clear to me that they really did want to be together, reflecting on what they were learning in the field, but the course's design at the time caused them to feel infantilized, as though they were being forced to waste their time in order to earn academic credit for work they found otherwise highly meaningful.

The assessment of Practicum surfaced a number of ways in which the course was missing the mark. First, Practicum claimed to be a place of integration, but nowhere did the program's description define what was to be integrated with what. Some believed that the small-group setting would be an ideal location for integrating the experiences students were having in the ministry field with the experiences they were undertaking in seminary classrooms and related academic work. However, activities in Practicum bore no resemblance to integration as defined in that way.

Second, Practicum included extensive check-ins every week, where students would share what they were experiencing in the field and receive feedback. While this practice could lead to many benefits, the check-ins were so long and involved that sessions sometimes ended immediately after everyone had shared. If one person was having a difficult time, the whole group would suspend its check-ins to help that person. This seemed beneficial in the moment, but it left students wondering whether Practicum was for learning or emotional support.

Finally, Practicum leadership presented the greatest challenge. The group of eleven instructors included some who had applied for the job I was starting. It also included several who had led Practicum groups for decades without adapting to the changes in the student body and the world of ministry. Among them were pastors who had retired many years previously and used Practicum as a setting for telling war stories, processing their own memories and grief at days gone by.

The redesign of the course took place in phases. First, we worked with a foundation to secure a grant related to creating programming around faith practices. Second, we suspended Practicum for one year while we carried out a new model, where each small group in which students participated focused on one faith practice as its theme. Themes included hospitality, discernment, and spiritual self-care. For each theme, a faculty member offered a guest lecture on how that practice informed their scholarship. In small groups, check-ins used the themes for the group as a guide for sharing, rather than using a check-in process with no structure or guardrails.

The grant-funded Practicum substitution had its high points and low points, but its main achievement was disrupting what had become an ingrown program that was giving integrative seminars a bad name on campus. The new form of Practicum that followed after the one-year, grant-funded break mirrored the grant-funded pilot.

A trefoil analysis of what needed to change would show that students needed some theological content to frame their sharing, creating an environment conducive to learning, rather than an emotional support group with participants who had signed up for something different and a facilitator untrained in support group leadership. Reflection was always strong in Practicum, but it required some rebalancing. As for horizon-expansion, faculty lectures gave students insights into the world of scholarship on faith, taking them inside the minds of professors with whom they were taking courses on other topics.

Curriculum Design

Over lunch with some students who had taken courses with me in the past, I asked if they had any suggestions for me, were I to create a new course. One student said she hoped to learn more about what it means to share leadership within a flat hierarchy, a topic we had touched on but not explored deeply. I took her up on her challenge and designed a new course. Below is an excerpt from its syllabus.

Course Description

Top-down, authoritarian practices doom organizations in a quickly changing world to stagnation, implode, or dismantle. Institutions that draw creative energy from all constituents, no matter their position in the hierarchy, are far more likely to thrive in today's leadership climate. What theories, practices, attitudes, and habits enable a leader to guide transformation and foster flourishing in a missional (or "mission-driven" or "transformation-oriented") movement or organization today? How can leaders recast their authority as a tool, encourage grassroots energy, share leadership across stakeholders, and bring out the best in a community? With a special emphasis on religious leadership and faith-based institutions, coupled with openness to leadership dynamics in any missional organization, this course will explore what makes for effective leadership within flat hierarchies during liminal seasons.

Course Objectives

Students who take this course will understand the differences between, and interrelatedness of:

- Power and authority; role clarity and "turf"
- Strategy and control
- Top-down and grassroots power
- Boundaries and relationship-building

They will be able to define for themselves what it means to be a religious leader and a professional serving a missional movement or organization.

Expectations

- Read required texts before course sessions
- Attend all course sessions in their entirety, embodying presence in affect and attitude
- Encourage the learning of other students in the course
- Complete assignments by or before deadlines
- Communicate with the instructor about any special needs or circumstances

Assignments

Online Participation: Biweekly Reading Reflections and Discussion, 50 percent

Beginning in the second week, Dean Drummond will post prompts every other week that encourage students to connect reading to leadership topics and questions. In the first week, they will write a reflection of 500 words to be shared with all. In the second, they will respond to no fewer than five classmates' reflections, building on their ideas.

Community Organizing Training and Reflection, 25 percent

Students will engage in six to eight hours of interreligious community organizing training through CONECT (Congregations Organized for a New Connecticut) or GHIAA (Greater Hartford Interfaith Action Alliance). Options will be made available to students by the second class meeting. Students will choose a training and then, subsequently, select an initiative supported by the community organizing coalition on which to write a case study (approx. 1,500 words), due the last day of class.

Take-Home Case Study Exam, 25 percent

Dean Drummond will write a fictional case study, accompanied by questions related to course material and concepts from community organizing training. The case will give students the opportunity to demonstrate their knowledge of key concepts and propose creative, strategic interventions that further the mission of the fictional institution.

The course's content and assignments align with the trefoil model. Students will learn theoretical frameworks for understanding leadership, including topics such as emotional systems, emergence, liberation theology, boundary management, and the missional movement. Students will gain exposure to social justice organizations in their communities, expanding their horizons beyond the campus. They will reflect on their readings, their experiences in community organizing training, and their evolving attitudes.

The trefoil model, used as a guide before the syllabus was even written, ensured a balanced course that provides both information and space for growth and integration.

An Organization Offering Lifelong Learning for Its Members

Many organizations choose themes for their program years or assign books for all members to read and discuss. While this shared learning impulse is commendable, reading alone does not foster transformation. It is the reflection on the reading and the discussions that challenge comfort zones that lead to meaningful attitudinal change. For these reasons, the trefoil model can ensure that organization-wide learning programs include the necessary components to foster not just new knowledge but also growth in participants' sense of purpose within the organization.

My family has traveled to an island off the coast of New Hampshire every summer for more than fifteen years, attending a family conference associated with our faith tradition. In an effort to build cohesion among the different organizations that host conferences on Star Island, the leadership introduced a summer theme last year. The theme was kindness. My role at the summer conference differs from my day job. During the year, I serve as the dean of a seminary, but on Star Island, I volunteer as the leader for the kids' chapel. I even learned how to play the ukulele just to lead the kids in music. While I am not very good at it—something the kids find amusing—I find it liberating.

Wanting to honor the summer's theme, I wrote a song for the children about kindness. Here are its lyrics:

We're Kind

By Sarah Drummond, for Star Island Kids

A car drives up beside you
The rain is pouring down
The driver doesn't see you, and
The splash could make you drown
You want to say, "Hey Buddy,
Watch the way you drive!"
But quickly you remember
It's enough to be alive. So you're kind.

Refrain:
Kind is not the same as "nice,"
It's better than being fair.
Kind is what we do for God
Who teaches us to care.
Jesus said a lot of things
The one to keep in mind
Is no matter what else we do
The main thing is... You're kind.

A bully on the playground
Cuts a place in line
You tell her you were first
And then she imitates your whine.
You know she's had a tough day
You failed that math test too
It's not okay she stole your spot
And you don't know what to do. So you're kind.

Refrain

Your brother stole your candy
That you had saved for weeks
He swears he was just trying to help
With chocolate in his cheeks.
"You had too much for one kid
The dentist would be rough
& an achy tummy's awful;
I thought you had enough." [long pause; frown]
So you're kind.

Refrain

Speak your truth (yeah!), say your piece (sure!),
Stand up for what is right.
But-when Christ said, "Love each other"
He likely meant, "Don't fight."
Kindness is our default move
It guides us to what's true.
From-there, we merely try our best
And-hope others will try too.

We're kind. Even when we're the only ones who even bother...
We're kind. Even when we don't wanner...
We're kind.
We're kind!

Star Island's theme program includes some attributes of the trefoil model, in differing proportions. Conferences chose books to read together, but not across the whole summer. Forays into personal reflection or lands beyond comfort zones varied from conference to conference. For me, writing a song for the first time since middle school, and playing an unfamiliar instrument in front of people who have no trouble expressing their preferences, resulted in a self-imposed expansion of horizons. The trefoil theoretical framework could provide organizations wishing to work with themes to build cohesion with simple, manageable guidance for program components that follow these themes while also being adaptable across constituencies.

An Individual Plotting a Path for Their Own Growth

Leaders of today and tomorrow must serve in part as leadership trainers for those in their care. They must share leadership among their constituents to build a broad enough base to effect meaningful change in their organizations, and they cannot assume that those constituents are adequately prepared to lead, even if they have previously carried significant responsibility. The first constituent a leader must be ready to train is themselves. The leader who is not intentionally growing in their skills, depth, and open-mindedness will not be able to motivate others to do the same. They will lack both empathy for how difficult learning to lead can be and the ability to model the vulnerability that encourages others to try something new.

Therefore, leaders must be ready to design plans for their own growth and talk openly about them with their constituencies. These plans can be broad and general, or they can focus on a specific set of skills the leader wants to develop. When making strategic plans for their organizations, leaders should include their own learning. The trefoil model provides a structure for ensuring balance and sustainability in that learning.

As I approach the end of an academic year and look forward to the next, I can use the trefoil model to describe my overall plans for learning and more specific approaches within that plan. I will teach a new course on sharing leadership in the missional organization.

One area I wish to learn more about before teaching this course is the psychology of teamwork, a subject I have never studied deeply. To address this, I signed up for a summer course on the topic. Between that and catching up on reading in my field, my need for informational content will be satisfied.

Next, I need to consider where I will find opportunities for reflective practice. I will continue to write my weekly theological reflection on leadership and connect intentionally with colleagues daily. However, the trefoil model reveals a gap in my life: I do not have a regular colleague group, and the professional organizations of which I am a member have scaled back offerings in that area. This gap, which the trefoil model helps me identify, motivates me to explore new options for reflective practice.

As for horizon expansion, one practice that helps me see beyond my sphere is volunteering as a peer accreditation evaluator. This fall, I will chair a peer evaluation team at a theological school that educates for a different religion. This experience will expose me to assumptions I take for granted as normative and help me imagine new ways of doing my own work.

Beyond the general lifelong learning that the trefoil model helps me plan, I can also use the model to grow in a specific set of skills I want to cultivate: consulting. I am occasionally asked to help organizations going through significant changes by offering consultation. Sometimes I am invited to speak, other times to listen and offer feedback. I have said yes to these invitations over the past fifteen years, but I have always felt I could and should be more intentional about this dimension of my work. The trefoil model provides a straightforward approach to leadership development for consulting without turning it into an overwhelming project, given my limited time.

First, I will read books and articles about how to offer consultations professionally, ethically, and effectively. Second, I will take time to reflect with peers who offer consulting services about building a practice that is both realistic within my demanding schedule and helpful to clients. I will gather both practical and technical advice and relational counsel on the potential pitfalls and benefits of this work. Third, I will explore the websites and materials of other consultants in my field to broaden my thinking about what I might be able to offer that is unique.

When a leader hears, "You need leadership development" or "You need some professional development for leadership," they might feel insulted. Such feelings are understandable, as feedback about the need for leadership development is often a passive-aggressive way of implying that a leader's skills are unsatisfactory. However, no one is fully prepared to lead in times like these, where unforeseeable challenges await around every corner. Therefore, a wise leader takes matters into their own hands, developing themselves and others without waiting for critical feedback.

Cultivating Competence

The Ministry of Leadership Development

The trefoil model for leadership development is simple, but its implementation need not be simplistic. The three areas of skills and content, reflective practice, and horizon expansion work together dynamically. Different areas of leadership development practices overlap and bleed into one another: Gaining a new skill broadens opportunities, and thus horizons; reflecting on experience causes a person to seek out new knowledge. The main benefit of using a trefoil structure for designing leadership development programs is that, once all three areas have received balanced attention, the one using the model has the basics covered and can now play.

Play, in this case, refers to the way in which human beings approach their activities imaginatively. Play causes a person to ask, "What would happen if...?" and take risks. One can only play when they feel free, rather than anxious as though under threat. Play is a low-risk simulation of life, where experimentation comes with no intolerable cost. It only happens, however, at the margins, in the space afforded for it. Those who are chronically overwhelmed have no space for play, because the stakes for where they place their time and attention are too high. Play is yet another reason why a leadership development protocol must be attainable, and leaders must make space for it in their own lives and in the lives of those whose leadership they are attempting to develop.

To break free from a sense of overwhelm, the leader can use the trefoil model even to design their play. Gain a skill that is impractical and unnecessary, just for fun. Engage in deep conversation with a stranger on a plane. Try something adventurous, or even scary. Such activities shake the leader loose from the sense that everything they do must be a means to an end, even though this playful protocol is indeed practical, as the unimaginative leader cannot formulate the needed new approaches for which this era calls.

The trefoil model must situate itself within a wider array of values in the human experience. It does not provide a whole way of life but rather a way of thinking about growth for leadership. An overall unhealthy person cannot engage it and expect that everything in their life will change. Certain transcendent life realities require care for leadership development to take root. If a person is developmentally stunted, uninterested in or unwilling to change, they might be able to grow in skills and knowledge, but not in depth of reflection or open-mindedness. Yet even stuntedness can be overcome.

When a person seeks to grow as a leader, but for whatever reason is not in a good enough place to engage in leadership development, they can focus on transcendent practices that improve the landscape on which their eventual leadership development can unfold. Such transcendent values include cultivating a positive attitude toward lifelong learning, developing spiritual practices that connect them with the divine, attending to loving relationships with friends and family, and engaging in bodily and emotional self-care.

Leadership development cannot take place in a vacuum. A person can only grow as a leader if they are, generally and overall, growing. The trefoil model for leadership development does not supplant transcendent values—positive attitudes, spiritual practices, loving relationships, and self-care—but rather helps the individual focus those values on their leadership in an attainable way. The institutional leader can use the trefoil model as a tool for supervision, staff development, and their own growth in leadership, but if they are generally inattentive to their own humanity, its usefulness will be limited.

Wonder and wherewithal, as opposed to apathy and abdication, are the traits that leadership development aspires to cultivate. The leader who approaches new challenges with curiosity, and addresses them using imagination that transforms problems into opportunities, will find psychological survival where others will not. Simple, attainable, and sustainable practices for lifelong learning will be essential for cultivating leaders with wonder and wherewithal.

Leaders must assume that they are not sufficiently prepared for the times. They must assume that they cannot work alone and must uplift other leaders around them, none of whom are prepared to lead either. Then, they must go about training themselves and others, rather than bemoaning ill-preparedness, as though some mythical educator in the past should have foreseen the unprecedented challenges of the day and prepared them for it. Bemoaning will not solve problems, but when one does not know what to do next, it can be a soothing option. The trefoil model helps the leader to know what to do now, and next.

NOTES

CHAPTER 1: THE OLD WAY WAS NO WAY

1 Augustine, *The City of God*, ed. F. W. Bussell, John Healey, and Ernest Barker (London: J.M. Dent & Sons, 1934).

2 adrienne maree brown, *Emergent Strategy: Shaping Change in a Changing World* (Chico, CA: AK Press, 2017).

3 brown, *Emergent Strategy*, 33.

4 Willie James Jennings, *After Whiteness: An Education in Belonging* (Grand Rapids, MI: Wm. B. Eerdmanns, 2020).

5 Susan Beaumont, *How to Lead When You Don't Know Where You Are Going: Leading in a Liminal Season* (Lanham, MD: Rowman & Littlefield, 2019).

6 Beaumont, *How to Lead*, 135.

7 See Beaumont, *How to Lead*, 156.

8 See Beaumont, *How to Lead*, 135.

9 Paulo Freire, *Pedagogy of the Oppressed*, trans. Myra Bergman Ramos (New York: Continuum, 1970).

10 This author does not believe that numerous courses on leadership should be required in seminary. Rather, she believes that practices of lifelong learning for leadership should begin in seminary and continue throughout one's ministry career.

11 *2020 Standards of Accreditation* (Pittsburgh: Association of Theological Schools, 2020), 4.3. https://www.ats.edu/files/galleries/standards-of-accreditation.pdf.

12 See Edward Farley, "Four Pedagogical Mistakes: A *Mea Culpa*," *Teaching Theology and Religion* 8, no. 4 (2005): 200-03.

13 A healthier response to fear of irrelevance on the part of those who teach abstract disciplines within the theological academy is to connect those disciplines with what is happening in religion now. Such engagement helps their students and broadens their scholarships' audience.

14 Scott Cormode, *Making Spiritual Sense: Christian Leaders as Spiritual Interpreters* (Nashville: Abingdon Press, 2006).
15 Gilbert Rendle, "Reclaiming Professional Jurisdiction: The Re-Emergence of the Theological Task of Ministry," *Theology Today* 59, no. 3 (2002): 408–20.
16 Rendle, "Reclaiming Professional Jurisdiction," 418.

CHAPTER 2: THE CHANGING CONTEXT FOR FAITH LEADERS

1 See Walter Earl Fluker, *The Ground Has Shifted: The Future of the Black Church in Post-Racial America* (New York: New York University Press, 2016).
2 See Justo L. González, *The History of Theological Education* (Nashville: Abingdon Press, 2015).
3 See Chris Argyris and Donald A. Schön, *Theory in Practice: Increasing Professional Effectiveness* (San Francisco: Jossey-Bass, 1974). Scholars of education for the professions argue that barriers to blending classroom-based and experiential learning come in the form of a "mismatch" (p. 187) regarding administration and expectations.
4 See William May, *Beleaguered Rulers: The Public Obligation of the Professional* (Louisville, KY: Westminster John Knox, 2001). In a chapter entitled "Ordained to What Public Purpose?," May suggests that the role of ministers across the Jewish and Christian traditions has come to include more convening than speaking for the divine, more "Prime Minister" than "President" (p. 240).
5 See Rendle, "Reclaiming Professional Jurisdiction."
6 The Memorial Church at Harvard University worships in the Christian tradition, although chapel life at Harvard Divinity School is interreligious in nature.
7 Katty Kay and Claire Shipman, *The Power Code: More Joy. Less Ego. More Impact for Women (and Everyone)* (New York: HarperCollins, 2023).
8 Doris Kearns Goodwin, *Leadership in Turbulent Times* (New York: Simon & Schuster, 2018).
9 Sam Jacobs, "The Choice," *TIME*, December 5, 2023.
10 Peter J. Gomes, *The Good Book: Reading the Bible with Mind and Heart* (New York: William Morrow, 1996).
11 Sarah Drummond, "Collapse," *Ministry Demystified* (blog), *Medium*, January 9, 2023, https://sbdrummond.medium.com/collapse-eeb53dac6d7b.

12 Robert Kegan, "Adult Development" (course, Harvard Graduate School of Education, Fall 1996). Diagram from Sarah Drummond, *Intentional Leadership In Between Seasons* (Cleveland, OH: Pilgrim Press, 2022), 81.

CHAPTER 3: A THEORETICAL FRAMEWORK FOR MINISTERIAL LEADERSHIP DEVELOPMENT

1 Robert D. Dale, *Leadership for a Changing Church: Charting the Shape of the River* (Nashville: Abingdon Press, 1998).
2 Dale, *Leadership for a Changing Church*, 18.
3 See Beaumont, *How to Lead*.
4 *Holmes–Pollock Letters: The Correspondence of Mr. Justice Holmes and Sir Frederick Pollock, 1874–1932*, ed. Mark DeWolfe Howe, 2nd ed. (Belknap Press, 1961), 109.
5 Mary Catherine Bateson, *Composing a Life* (New York: Atlantic Monthly, 1989).
6 Edwin H. Friedman, *A Failure of Nerve: Leadership in the Age of the Quick Fix*, ed. Margaret M. Treadwell and Edward W. Beal (New York: Seabury Books, 2007).
7 Arthur P. Boers, *Never Call Them Jerks: Healthy Responses to Difficult Behavior* (Bethesda, MD: Alban Institute, 1999).
8 brown, *Emergent Strategy*, 52.

CHAPTER 4: LEADERSHIP DEVELOPMENT THROUGH CONVEYING KNOWLEDGE, INFORMATION, AND SKILLS

1 See Paul Tillich, *The Courage to Be* (New Haven, CT: Yale University Press, 1952).
2 See Parker J. Palmer, *The Active Life: A Spirituality of Work, Creativity, and Caring* (San Francisco: Jossey-Bass, 1990; repr., 1999), 15.
3 *2020 Standards of Accreditation*.
4 I consider in the work of my colleague Hi'ilea Hobart, an anthropologist who writes about food, whose recent book *Cooling the Tropics* considers the intersection of colonialism and refrigeration in Hawai'i. Topics that make strange bedfellows are the new "originality." See Hi'lei Hobart, *Cooling the Tropics: Ice, Indigeneity, and Hawai'ian Refreshment* (Durham, NC: Duke University Press, 2022).
5 Donald A. Schön, *Educating the Reflective Practitioner* (San Francisco: Jossey Bass, 1987).

6 Schön, *Educating the Reflective Practitioner*, 13.

7 Argyris and Schön, *Theory in Practice: Increasing Professional Effectiveness*.

8 Argyris and Schön, *Theory in Practice: Increasing Professional Effectiveness*, 12: "This [false dichotomy] suggests that skill learning and theory learning are different kinds of activities; it suggests further that theory learning may be appropriately undertaken in one kind of place (school) and skill learning in another (work)."

9 Schön, *Educating the Reflective Practitioner*, 39.

10 Argyris and Schön, *Theory in Practice: Increasing Professional Effectiveness*, 146–47.

11 See Sarah Drummond, "A Hardworking Protestant's Unease with 'Ease,'" *Reflections* (Spring 2024), https://reflections.yale.edu/article/ghost-machine-ethics-ai/hardworking-protestant-s-unease-ease.

12 Art Kleiner, *The Wise Advocate: The Inner Voice of Strategic Leadership*, ed. Jeffrey Schwartz, Josie Thomson, and Jonathan Yen (Old Saybrook, CT: Tantor Media, 2019).

CHAPTER 5: LEADERSHIP DEVELOPMENT THROUGH FOSTERING THEOLOGICAL REFLECTION

1 John Patton, *From Ministry to Theology: Pastoral Action and Reflection* (Nashville: Abingdon Press, 1995), 23.

2 Kenneth H. Pohly, *Transforming the Rough Places: The Ministry of Supervision*, 2nd ed. (Franklin, TN: Providence House, 2001).

3 L. Gregory Jones and Kevin R. Armstrong, *Resurrecting Excellence: Shaping Faithful Christian Ministry* (Grand Rapids, MI: Eerdmans, 2006), 118.

4 Dudley Rose served as Associate Dean at Harvard Divinity School and Senior Pastor of North Prospect UCC from 1995 to 2020 and mentored many students, including this author.

5 Kegan, "Adult Development."

6 Catherine C. Tran and Sandra Hughes Boyd, *Spiritual Discovery: A Method for Discernment in Small Groups and Congregations* (Lanham, MD: Rowman & Littlefield, 2016).

7 Jeffrey H. Mahan, Barbara B. Troxell, and Carol J. Allen, *Shared Wisdom: A Guide to Case Study Reflection in Ministry* (Nashville: Abingdon Press, 1993).

8 Stephen Lewis, Matthew Wesley Williams, and Dori Grinenko Baker, *Another Way: Living and Leading Change On-Purpose* (Nashville: Chalice Press, 2020).
9 Robert Kegan and Lisa Laskow Lahey, *Immunity to Change: How to Overcome It and Unlock the Potential in Yourself and Your Organization* (Boston: Harvard Business Press, 2009).
10 Diane M. Millis, *Conversation—The Sacred Art: Practicing Presence in the Age of Distraction* (Woodstock, VT: Skylight Paths, 2013).

CHAPTER 6: LEADERSHIP DEVELOPMENT THROUGH EXPANDING HORIZONS

1 Merriam and Caffarella, *Learning in Adulthood: A Comprehensive Guide*, 321.
2 Pohly, "Transforming the Rough Places."
3 The author worked with a spiritual director who used Keating's methods, Barbara Prendergast, from 2000 to 2005 in Milwaukee, Wisconsin. During that same time frame, she studied Welcoming Prayer with Jesuit spiritual teacher Mary Dwyer.
4 Millis, *Conversation—The Sacred Art.*
5 Peter Neville Rule, *Dialogue and Boundary Learning: Educational Futures, Rethinking Theory and Practice* (Rotterdam: SensePublishers, 2015).
6 brown, *Emergent Strategy*, 41.
7 Matt Baillie Smith and Nina Laurie, "International Volunteering and Development: Global Citizenship and Neoliberal Professionalisation Today," *Transactions of the Institute of British Geographers* 36, no. 4 (2011): 545–59, 551. http://www.jstor.org/stable/23020828.
8 Joyce E. Bono, Winny Shen, and Mark Snyder, "Fostering Integrative Community Leadership," *Leadership Quarterly* 21, no. 2 (2010): 324–35. https://doi.org/10.1016/j.leaqua.2010.01.010.
9 Ann Curry-Stevens, "New Forms of Transformative Education Pedagogy for the Privileged," *Journal of Transformative Education* 5, no. 1 (2007): 33–58, 38 table 1.
10 Alun David Morgan, "Journeys into Transformation: Travel to an 'Other' Place as a Vehicle for Transformative Learning," *Journal of Transformative Education* 8, no. 4 (2010): 246-68.
11 Morgan, "Journeys into Transformation," 247.
12 Morgan, "Journeys into Transformation."

13 Anu Taranath, *Beyond Guilt Trips: Mindful Travel in an Unequal World* (Toronto: Between the Lines, 2019), 12.
14 Taranath, *Beyond Guilt Trips*, 18.
15 Taranath, *Beyond Guilt Trips*, 17.
16 Taranath, *Beyond Guilt Trips*, 156.
17 Taranath, *Beyond Guilt Trips*, 115.
18 Taranath, *Beyond Guilt Trips*, 124.
19 Taranath, *Beyond Guilt Trips*, 203.
20 Taranath, *Beyond Guilt Trips*, 148.
21 Taranath, *Beyond Guilt Trips*, 28.
22 Camila Vieira Müller et al., "Volunteer Tourism, Transformative Learning and Its Impacts on Careers: The Case of Brazilian Volunteers," *International Journal of Tourism Research* 22, no. 6 (2020): 726–38. https://doi.org/10.1002/jtr.2368.

BIBLIOGRAPHY

2020 Standards of Accreditation (Pittsburgh: Association of Theological Schools, 2020). https://www.ats.edu/files/galleries/standards-of-accreditation.pdf.

Argyris, Chris, and Donald A. Schön. *Theory in Practice: Increasing Professional Effectiveness.* San Francisco: Jossey-Bass, 1974.

Augustine. *The City of God.* Edited by F. W. Bussell, John Healey, and Ernest Barker. London: J. M. Dent & Sons, 1934.

Bateson, Mary Catherine. *Composing a Life.* New York: Atlantic Monthly, 1989.

Beaumont, Susan. *How to Lead When You Don't Know Where You Are Going: Leading in a Liminal Season.* Lanham, MD: Rowman & Littlefield, 2019.

Boers, Arthur P. *Never Call Them Jerks: Healthy Responses to Difficult Behavior.* Bethesda, MD: Alban Institute, 1999.

Bono, Joyce E., Winny Shen, and Mark Snyder. "Fostering Integrative Community Leadership." *Leadership Quarterly* 21, no. 2 (2010): 324-35. https://doi.org/10.1016/j.leaqua.2010.01.010.

brown, adrienne maree. *Emergent Strategy: Shaping Change in a Changing World.* Chico, CA: AK Press, 2017.

Cormode, Scott. *Making Spiritual Sense: Christian Leaders as Spiritual Interpreters.* Nashville: Abingdon Press, 2006.

Curry-Stevens, Ann. "New Forms of Transformative Education Pedagogy for the Privileged." *Journal of Transformative Education* 5, no. 1 (2007): 33-58.

Dale, Robert D. *Leadership for a Changing Church: Charting the Shape of the River.* Nashville: Abingdon Press, 1998.

Drummond, Sarah, "Collapse." *Ministry Demystified* (blog). *Medium*, January 9, 2023. https://sbdrummond.medium.com/collapse-eeb53dac6d7b.

Drummond, Sarah. "A Hardworking Protestant's Unease with 'Ease'." *Reflections* (Spring 2024). https://reflections.yale.edu/article/ghost-machine-ethics-ai/hardworking-protestant-s-unease-ease.

———. *Intentional Leadership in between Seasons.* Cleveland, OH: Pilgrim Press, 2022.

Farley, Edward. "Four Pedagogical Mistakes: A *Mea Culpa.*" *Teaching Theology and Religion* 8, no. 4 (2005): 200-03.

Fluker, Walter Earl. *The Ground Has Shifted: The Future of the Black Church in Post-Racial America.* New York: New York University Press, 2016.

Freire, Paulo. *Pedagogy of the Oppressed.* Translated by Myra Bergman Ramos. New York: Continuum, 1970.

Friedman, Edwin H. *A Failure of Nerve: Leadership in the Age of the Quick Fix.* Edited by Margaret M. Treadwell and Edward W. Beal. New York: Seabury Books, 2007. http://www.loc.gov/catdir/toc/ecip072/2006033685.html.

Gomes, Peter J. *The Good Book: Reading the Bible with Mind and Heart.* New York: William Morrow, 1996.

González, Justo L. *The History of Theological Education.* Nashville: Abingdon Press, 2015.

Goodwin, Doris Kearns. *Leadership in Turbulent Times.* New York: Simon & Schuster, 2018.

Hobart, Hiʻlei. *Cooling the Tropics: Ice, Indigeneity, and Hawaiʻian Refreshment.* Durham, NC: Duke University Press, 2022.

Jacobs, Sam. "The Choice." *TIME*, December 5, 2023.

Jennings, Willie James. *After Whiteness: An Education in Belonging.* Grand Rapids, MI: Eerdmanns, 2020.

Jones, L. Gregory, and Kevin R. Armstrong. *Resurrecting Excellence: Shaping Faithful Christian Ministry.* Grand Rapids, MI: Eerdmans, 2006.

Kay, Katty, and Claire Shipman. *The Power Code: More Joy. Less Ego. More Impact for Women (and Everyone).* New York: HarperCollins, 2023.

Kegan, Robert, and Lisa Laskow Lahey. *Immunity to Change: How to Overcome It and Unlock the Potential in Yourself and Your Organization.* Boston: Harvard Business Press, 2009.

Kleiner, Art. *The Wise Advocate: The Inner Voice of Strategic Leadership.* Edited by Jeffrey Schwartz, Josie Thomson, and Jonathan Yen. Old Saybrook, CT: Tantor Media, 2019.

Lewis, Stephen, Matthew Wesley Williams, and Dori Grinenko Baker. *Another Way: Living and Leading Change On-Purpose.* Nashville: Chalice Press, 2020.

Mahan, Jeffrey H., Barbara B. Troxell, and Carol J. Allen. *Shared Wisdom: A Guide to Case Study Reflection in Ministry.* Nashville: Abingdon Press, 1993.

May, William. *Beleaguered Rulers: The Public Obligation of the Professional.* Louisville, KY: Westminster John Knox, 2001.

Merriam, Sharan B., and Rosemary S. Caffarella. *Learning in Adulthood: A Comprehensive Guide.* San Francisco: John Wiley and Sons, 1999.

Millis, Diane M. *Conversation—The Sacred Art: Practicing Presence in the Age of Distraction.* Woodstock, VT: Skylight Paths, 2013.

Morgan, Alun David. "Journeys into Transformation: Travel to an 'Other' Place as a Vehicle for Transformative Learning." *Journal of Transformative Education* 8, no. 4 (2010): 246-68.

Müller, Camila Vieira, Müller Camila Vieira, Scheffer Angela Beatriz Busato, and Closs Lisiane Quadrado. "Volunteer Tourism, Transformative Learning and Its Impacts on Careers: The Case of Brazilian Volunteers." *The International Journal of Tourism Research* 22, no. 6 (2020–2019): 726-38. https://doi.org/10.1002/jtr.2368.

Palmer, Parker J. *The Active Life: A Spirituality of Work, Creativity, and Caring.* San Francisco: Jossey-Bass, 1990.

Patton, John. *From Ministry to Theology: Pastoral Action and Reflection.* Nashville: Abingdon Press, 1995.

Pohly, Kenneth H. *Transforming the Rough Places: The Ministry of Supervision.* 2nd ed. Franklin, TN: Providence House, 2001.

Rendle, Gilbert. "Reclaiming Professional Jurisdiction: The Re-Emergence of the Theological Task of Ministry." *Theology Today* 59, no. 3 (2002): 408–20.

Rule, Peter Neville. *Dialogue and Boundary Learning.* Educational Futures, Rethinking Theory and Practice, vol. 66. Rotterdam: SensePublishers, 2015.

Schön, Donald A. *Educating the Reflective Practitioner.* San Francisco: Jossey Bass, 1987.

Smith, Matt Baillie, and Nina Laurie. "International Volunteering and Development: Global Citizenship and Neoliberal Professionalisation Today." *Transactions of the Institute of British Geographers* 36, no. 4 (2011): 545-59.

Taranath, Anu. *Beyond Guilt Trips: Mindful Travel in an Unequal World.* Toronto: Between The Lines, 2019.

Tillich, Paul. *The Courage to Be.* New Haven, CT: Yale University Press, 1952.

Tran, Catherine C., and Sandra Hughes Boyd. *Spiritual Discovery: A Method for Discernment in Small Groups and Congregations.* Lanham, MD: Rowman & Littlefield, 2016.

INDEX